BUILDING TOWN
and
COUNTRY CHURCHES

BUILDING TOWN
and
COUNTRY CHURCHES

By

Harold Longenecker

MOODY PRESS
CHICAGO

Original title: *The Village Church: Its Pastor and Program*

Contents

Foreword

HAROLD LONGENECKER is eminently equipped to write this book.

He has a heart for the 60 million people who live in town and country America. He has preached to them and worked with them. He writes with authority based on experience.

He knows the Word of God and what it has to say about the church. Here is no man-made program. Instead, here is a God-given approach to the winning of souls and the building of the local church. Harold Longenecker is no impractical mystic, but neither is he an advocate of "Christian salesmanship." He gives us a beautiful balance of spiritual vision and practical insight. The Christian burdened for rural ministry cannot help but find just the information—and inspiration—he needs in the pages of this book.

I like the way the author dignifies the work of the pastor in the smaller community—and rightly so! Not everyone is called to a ministry in the big cities, and the man called to the rural church must remember that every church is big in the eyes of God.

By showing us the importance of the town and country ministry and by explaining how this ministry can be done effectively, Harold Longenecker has filled a great need; and for this I am grateful. Those of us ministering in the metropolitan areas need his forceful reminder that church planting is not a matter of either/or but both/and: we need the work in the cities and we need the work in the town and country areas.

I pray that God's Spirit will use this concise manual to challenge and help train a dedicated army of Christians who will take the gospel to the overlooked areas of our land.

WARREN W. WIERSBE

Moody Memorial Church
Chicago, Illinois

Preface

MANY DIFFERENT KINDS of evangelistic societies have been formed in response to America's spiritual needs. City missions, orphanages, children's missions, youth organizations, Christian schools, Sunday schools, and church associations have been instituted for the purpose of reaching the unreached. Working sacrificially, and many times without publicity or headlines, these groups have been successful in making a forceful impact on many thousands of neglected people.

This book is dedicated to a select group, to those who are at work in small town America, particularly to those whose ministry is dedicated to the development of the local church. My purpose is to set forth some principles relating to the founding and growth of town and country churches, so that others may find help in this important ministry.

Distressingly little has been written on this point; and aside from a few noted exceptions, our schools and seminaries have not given much attention to this need. One rural pastor, after a number of years on the field, has this to say about his preparation for the ministry: "I am amazed when I think of the little help that my training in the seminary was in meeting the real problems with which I was confronted in these churches. My teachers helped me in the study of the Bible, church history, and in the preparation of sermons, and made a few suggestions concerning pastoral work. But I must say, in the light of years spent in grappling with real problems in small towns and open country, that the training I received in seminary was very limited."[1] It is only fair to add that some educators have recognized this deficiency and are taking steps to remedy it. However, the remedies are neither as satisfactory nor as widely applied as they ought to be.

I offer this work, therefore, because I believe there is a need for it; and I hope what is written here may be helpful to the missionary pastor who has dedicated himself to this important task.

1

The Local Church Under Attack

THE LOCAL CHURCH is under attack. Sometimes the opposition is subtle, as evident in some of the books and magazine articles which feature proposals for a fundamental restructuring of the church. Other pressures are more open and scathing. The exponents of the "radical left" do not hide their intentions to destroy organized religion. The institution of the church, along with all other institutions which are indigenous to western civilization, is to be dismantled.

Destructive pressures do not come only from exponents of change. Some who claim to be evangelical Christians unwittingly assert a negative influence. The "non-institutional" church, which recently has become prominent, seems on the surface to be a rather harmless and spontaneous form of Christian expression. But the movement is so lacking in compliance with the standards of church life as spelled out in the New Testament that we have good reason to inquire as to its ultimate destination. And many other Christians, who have no affinity with any radical movement, likewise are lending their influence to the pressures against the church by the simple fact that they know so little about it, have such low-grade concepts of its importance, and are so ineffective in its support. Put all these factors together, and the attack upon the church assumes mountainous proportions.

For this reason it is necessary to think through some of the biblical concepts concerning the local church. The tendency

11

to disregard the local church has become so pervasive that it is impossible to write on any theme having to do with church life without spelling out the foundation from which one approaches the subject.

The purpose of this first chapter is to survey the testimony of the Word of God on this important issue. Several questions naturally arise as one considers the present climate in religious circles. Does the local church have any real reason to exist? What is the local church? What are the functions of a local church? These questions, all of which grow out of the present religious ferment, find their answers in a survey of New Testament teaching. The New Testament anticipates these very questions and establishes beyond question the *validity* of the local church, the *nature* of the local church, and the *functions* of the local church.

THE VALIDITY OF THE LOCAL CHURCH

A discussion of the church in a biblical context must begin by a study of the church in its universal form. The church in its *local* form is both an organism and an *organization*. The church in its *universal* form is only an *organism*.

The latter concept of the church is a key point in New Testament doctrine. One cannot treat fairly the epistle of Paul to the Ephesians without recognizing the fundamentally important place which the universal church holds in the Christian scheme of truth. Every Christian is a member of that church. Paul speaks of it as the body of Christ. He tells us in 1 Corinthians 12:13 that we are baptized into this body, apparently at the moment of conversion. This great mystical entity knows no geographic or ecclesiological boundaries, and therefore provides us with the highest possible concept of the relationship of all believers of the present age to the living Christ Himself. While our emphasis here is on the local church, we must establish at the outset that the local church concept draws its impetus from the fundamental truth of the church as the body of Christ.

But while most people in evangelical circles respond warmly to the truth of the *universal* church, the response is not nearly so emphatic to the truth of the *local* church. Yet the New Testament is as insistent on the one as on the other. In short, the New Testament clearly establishes the validity of the local church.

Argument may be drawn first of all from the study of the word itself. With respect to its biblical origins, Scofield tells us that it is derived from a compound Greek word composed of *ek* meaning out of, and *kaleo* meaning to call. Thus *church* means an assembly of called-out ones.[1]

In this connection, it is interesting to make a careful study of this word in the New Testament. It is used several times in its classical Greek sense, such as Acts 7:38, where Stephen speaks of the church in the wilderness. It is used at least twelve times in reference to the universal church. But it is used over ninety times in its singular or plural form, in reference to the local assembly. We may thus conclude that the apostles gave very sustained attention to this divinely established organization. It is true that frequency of reference does not establish the importance of a doctrine, but one can scarcely view the amount of space given by New Testament writers to the subject of the local church without concluding that it was for them a very important concept indeed.[2]

But argument may also be drawn from the practice of the apostles. Acts 13 and 14 seem to constitute a prototype of what God's missionary enterprise was meant to be. It was the first formal, planned, extensive missionary venture of the early church. And here again the local church comes into prominent view. First, the missionary enterprise proceeded from a local church. The church at Antioch spawned this missionary venture. That young church, which was itself the

outgrowth of the missionary movement from Jerusalem, became a dominant sending agency. Here the Spirit of God
began his work by calling Paul and Barnabas for the special
task of world missions. The leaders in Antioch responded
obediently, set Paul and Barnabas apart, and commissioned
them for their divinely appointed task. Thus this first important missionary venture issues from a local church.

It is equally plain that it resulted in the formation of other
local churches. Paul went forth with the burning desire to
evangelize. He preached both in synagogues and outside of
synagogues. He preached in streets and in buildings. Always
his purpose was to evangelize. That was his immediate goal.
But beyond this immediate goal, Paul was motivated by an
intense desire to establish these new believers in local visible
fellowships. After he had reached Derbe, the farthest point
of his first journey, he retraced his steps to exhort the brethren
and strengthen them in their faith.

Acts 14:21-23 recounts this important segment of church-
building history. When Paul returned to these cities, he
found the "church" already in existence (note v. 23). We are
also informed that he ordained elders in every church, which
indicates a certain simple, organizational procedure. It seems
safe to conclude, therefore, that the apostle Paul had as his
ultimate goal the establishment of local indigenous churches.
The mission enterprise which proceeded *from* a local church
also resulted in the formation of *other* local churches. Thus
the validity of the local church is borne out by the New Testament missionary enterprise.

A final argument for the validity of the local church may be
seen in the detailed instructions given by New Testament
writers to the young churches and pastors of that era. In
Ephesians, Philippians, and Colossians—the great church
epistles—there are many important references to church polity
and to the responsibilities of church leaders. This emphasis

becomes much more detailed as Paul writes his epistles to Titus and Timothy. There the Great Church Planter lays out the qualifications for church officers, the types of offices which the local church should have, their responsibilities and how they are to be chosen. This instruction would not likely have been included in inspired Scriptures if the local assembly was not strategically important in God's program. If only the universal body of Christ existed, Paul's teaching in these books could have been dispensed with. We may, therefore, properly view this area of biblical teaching as another argument for the validity and the scriptural authenticity of the local church.

The Nature of the Local Church

A second question which arises in any discussion of the visible church has to do with its nature. How does one define the church? What is it in essence?

Generally, in respect to the universal church, it may be described as the localized and visible expression of the mystical body of Christ. One writer says that "local churches are points of consciousness and activity for the great all-inclusive unit." He also says that "the local church is a microcosm, a specialized localization of the universal body."[3] A comparison has been made of the universal church to the Gulf Stream. The Gulf Stream is a vast, generally invisible movement of water through the Atlantic Ocean exerting great effects on both land masses of North America and Europe. Yet it is not easily distinguished. It has no shore line.[4] On the other hand, the local, visible church can be likened to the Mississippi River which has plainly defined banks, with a clearly outlined course, and a very distinct structure.

Specifically, we may define the nature of the local organized church from a careful study of the New Testament. A review of the writings of New Testament authors makes it clear that

a New Testament church is marked by the following characteristics:

1. It is composed of a group of confessing Christians. There
   is no New Testament evidence that people were members
   of the church without having openly confessed Jesus
   Christ as Lord and Saviour.

2. These Christians meet together in one geographic area.
   It is possible that the church at Rome, for example, while
   being viewed as a single church, may have met in several
   localities, but this does not refute the inference that a
   visible church usually is made up of confessing Christians
   in one geographic area who meet together in that place.

3. Christians meet together the first day of the week. There
   seems to be no indication of any standard regarding the
   time of this meeting. Christians have met very early in
   the Lord's Day or very late at night. Today the American
   church meets rather uniformly at 11:00 Sunday morning.
   But the time is immaterial. The important thing is that
   Christians meet together the first day of the week, in com-
   memoration of the resurrection of Jesus Christ.

4. Christians meet together to keep the ordinances of bap-
   tism and the Lord's Supper. Believers who confess Jesus
   Christ are baptized in water, signifying death to sin and
   self and union with Jesus Christ. These same Christians
   periodically partake of the bread and the cup as symbols
   of the broken body and shed blood of the Lord Jesus
   Christ. This exercise constitutes a communion service.

5. These people exercise biblical church discipline. The
   local church, under the leadership of elders and deacons,
   takes whatever action may be necessary to maintain the
   testimony of the fellowship by removing from visible and
   organizational membership those who are compromising
   the faith.

6. These people serve together under the leadership of biblical officers, known in the Bible as deacons and elders. These elders and deacons are spoken of from the very earliest times of church history, and their responsibility is clearly defined and a method of choice plainly outlined. It seems that a New Testament church authentically operates as a church when these officers are exercising their proper responsibilities.

7. Christians form an organized group in which the gifts of the Spirit may be exercised. The New Testament seems to indicate a difference between "sign" gifts and "ministry" gifts. It is this writer's opinion that the sign gifts of the Holy Spirit referred to in the New Testament were temporary rather than permanent, and that the local church is to be the forum in which the ministry gifts are to be exercised.

8. The people who constitute the local church meet together for the purpose of fulfilling the functions of the church.

With this as a background, we can construct a working definition of a local New Testament church. It is *a group of confessing Christians, in one geographic area, meeting together the first day of the week for the purpose of fellowship, teaching, worship, and testimony, keeping the ordinances, exercising discipline, recognizing their spiritual leaders, and ministering through the gifts bestowed by the Spirit of God, for the purpose of fulfilling the functions of a New Testament church.*

It is most important that we grasp the essentials that are here outlined. There is plenty of room for rethinking the functions and the structure of the local church today. Many present practices are carried over from previous eras and are of very little contemporary relevance. But in any restructuring of the local church, New Testament standards must not be violated. Dr. Francis Schaeffer has written very clearly on this subject, and I recommend his book, *The Church at the End of the Twentieth Century.*[5] We must learn to distinguish between the forms and the freedoms of the local church. And an enlightened discussion of our freedoms is only possible as we understand the forms.

THE FUNCTIONS OF THE LOCAL CHURCH

One question remains to be considered: What do local churches do? More importantly, what does the New Testament *require* local churches to do?

By careful consideration of the New Testament teaching, we may gather the following suggestions. Local churches meet together in the weekly assembly to pray, to teach, to worship, to choose leaders, to hear the preaching and teaching of the Word, to keep the ordinances, to communicate material things to others, to share their testimonies with each other, to discipline erring members, and to perform acts of charity for the household of God and for all men. Beyond this, local churches join together in mutually cooperative ventures with other churches, and confer together on important issues (Ac 15).

All of these may be summed up, however, in just a few categories. Churches should meet together for worship and fellowship, to hear teaching and preaching, and to exercise the functions of a viable organization. These functions include the election of officers, the maintenance of discipline, and the performance of rountine business. These are the things that should happen when churches meet.

But what is the purpose behind these meetings? Are the meetings in the church an end in themselves, or do these meetings take place so that something else can happen? This brings us to a very crucial issue—one that needs to be simply stated and pointedly emphasized. The New Testament teaches that the local church meets together so that the *individuals* within that local church may be equipped for fulfilling their responsibility in world evangelization.

The popular statement that "the supreme task of the church is the evangelization of the world" is true and yet subject to much misinterpretation. Under the repetition of that statement, many Christians have abdicated personal responsibility and have assigned the task of world evangelization to the impersonal group called "the church." Shall missionaries be sent to the far corners of the world? Then let the church do it. Is money needed for missions? Then let the church give it. Should more praying be done for the work of God? Then let the church pray.

The New Testament gives us no authority for thinking of evangelism as the responsibility of some group, *as a group,* even if that group is the church. When Jesus Christ gave the commission to his followers—in Luke 24, in Matthew 28, in John 21, or in Acts 1:8—it is always given to *individuals.* It was to individuals that he gave the task of world evangelization, for the church was not yet formed. Individuals must evangelize men—here at home, across the backyard fence, in the factory in which men work, in the next state, in a distant part of our hemisphere, or in a remote part of the world. Individuals will have to do this. It is true that all the individuals which constitute the church will have a part in this program, but it is not an impersonal, corporate body that is going to do the job. It will be done when individuals get busy and do it.

This truth is supported by Scripture. In Ephesians 4:11-12, Paul expressly teaches that the purpose behind Christ's gifts to the church was that the saints of God should be equipped for the ministry. These gifts are given "for the equipping of the saints for the work of service" (NASB). In 2 Timothy 2:2, Paul speaking to Timothy says, "the things which thou hast heard of me among many witnesses, the same commit thou to faithful men who shall be able to teach others also." A practical illustration of how this will work out in a local church program is found in Acts 19, in the phenomenal story of the church at Ephesus. There, for two years, Paul led this church in a teaching program which finally resulted in the evangelization of the whole Asiatic peninsula. The ingredients are implicit in the incident itself. Paul's teaching ministry was stationary. He taught, and taught, and retaught. And those who had been taught went out from Ephesus to teach others, who in turn taught others, who in turn evangelized the area known as Asia Minor.

We must comprehend this point clearly. If we do not, we are in danger of perpetuating several serious errors. First, we will leave the impression that an impersonal group of some kind is responsible for evangelism while the average Christian foots the bill. Also, we will perpetuate the idea that the church exists *primarily* to get sinners inside the building so that they can hear the Word of God and get saved.

Now, while it is necessary for Christians to pay the bill for evangelism, and while it is perfectly acceptable for sinners to get saved inside of church buildings, we must understand that this is not the primary objective of the church. The church does not meet together to provide a forum for evangelism. It meets together *to equip the saints* for the work of evangelism. Between those two concepts there is fixed a very wide gulf—one that is not easily bridged. Yet, if we intend to give the church renewed potency, we have no recourse but to thoroughly get hold of this concept and then to put it into practice in every stratum of church life.

How does all of this relate to the proposition with which I began this chapter, notably that the church is under siege? The application is direct and explicit. The church cannot defend itself against the forces arrayed against her today if she is not sure that she has a biblical right to exist: the *validity* of the church must be established. If we do not understand what the local church is, then our churches will be susceptible to every aberration of religious thought, and the end result will be immobilization, if not ruin: the *nature* of the church must be seen clearly. Finally, if the church does not know what her *objective* is, she simply cannot do her work. I suggest therefore that a careful review of the validity of the New Testament church, the precise nature of the church, and the biblical objective of the church will go a long way toward helping us develop a vigorous and much needed "local church apologetic."

2

The Importance of the Town and Country Church

WE HAVE DISCOVERED that the local church is important. But what about the local small-town church?

The question must be faced and answered. If the rural church is unimportant, then let's forget about it. But if it is important, then proper steps should be taken to correct the present unhealthy situation.

This book is being written by one who firmly believes that the town and country church is not only important, but absolutely essential to the total spiritual well-being of our nation. The great expansive rural areas of the United States, and the churches that dot its landscape, cannot blithely be written off without subsequent spiritual loss. From these areas this nation has drawn its strength. Rural and small town America has left its indelible imprint upon us. And though our culture is changing with each passing year, there is no doubt that a rural America will continue to exist and to exert its influence upon us.

But what of the church in rural America? What of its history? From whence has it come? What has been its contribution? What is its present status? What of its need? These questions face an honest and concerned inquirer, and demand an answer.

HISTORICAL PERSPECTIVE

Perhaps a somewhat nostalgic review of the past will be helpful. Let's listen first to Mark Dawber: "It is easy in these days to laugh at the rigidity of puritan ecclesiasticism, but it contributed something to America which possibly never before was used as a foundation for building a new civilization."[1] While we must not place halos on the heads of our forefathers, an honest appraisal of their spiritual contributions should make us hang our heads in shame. Commenting on early American religious practices, H. K. Rowe says: "Pastors of parish churches felt an obligation to itinerate at intervals among remote settlements. As earlier evangelists . . . had gone among the Indians of Massachusetts, . . . so in the last half of the eighteenth century zealous preachers visited Cape Cod, pushed their way up into the granite hills of New Hampshire, and traveled along the inlets and the rocky shore of Maine. Such men went at their own charges, rode their own horses, and lodged as hospitality offered. . . . These men endured hardships on starvation salaries because of their religious devotion."[2]

Dawber comments on the extent and outreach of early efforts:

"As the pioneers penetrated and cleared the wilderness . . . they established their places of worship . . . where God's law was proclaimed. Jonathan Edwards' famous pulpit dissertation on 'Sinners in the Hands of an Angry God' was . . . a . . . truth which was proclaimed from one end of the colonies to the other."[3]

But the spiritual need of the colonies was not only met by the ministries of individuals preachers. Societies and mission boards, dedicated to mission work on the frontier, were successfully organized. In 1801 the Congregationalists and Presbyterians formed a union to reach the pioneers with the gospel. In 1813 the Massachusetts and Connecticut missionary societies sent out investigators to look over the field and later sent out 200 missionaries and established 400 churches. In 1824 the well-known American Sunday School Union was born. The American Home Mission Society, a union of Presbyterians, Reformed, and Congregational churches, was organized in 1826. Still later, in 1832, the Baptist Home Missionary Society was formed.

From this beginning the village church in America progressed to the point where it became a recognized force in American Christianity. Many elderly persons who were reared in rural America can recall when virtually the entire community would go to church on the Lord's Day. Some would walk miles to get there. Rural preachers gave themselves with earnestness to their task. The Spirit of God was often present in a unique fashion. People were soundly converted, and Christians were built up in the faith.

But several factors began to emerge simultaneously, creating an entirely different religious climate.

Economically, the machine age set in, and rural America experienced revolutionary industrial development. More and more machines took the place of hand laborers. Fewer workers were required to harvest the crops. Farm population began to decline. Some folks moved to the city. A few widely scattered and remote communities died.

On the religious scene, other events occurred. Ministerial students began to acquire higher education. A trend toward bigger and more highly organized churches developed. Full pastoral support was pressed upon many country churches which had never before operated on this basis. Many church leaders made an effort to conform rural church practices to those of the city.

These conditions, taken together, could not help but make a forceful impact on village church life. First, there was a decline in church attendance. And declining church attendance resulted in declining offerings. This in turn meant that, if the ideal of the fully supported ministry was to be maintained, several churches would have to share one pastor. Thus, the practice of the "part-time" church was encouraged, and what are known in some areas as three-quarter, half- and quarter-time churches sprang up. Then resulted a still further reduction of interest, producing an even greater curtailment of activities. Many churches eventually ended up altogether closed or else maintained themselves at some irreducible minimum by the sheer determination of one or two hardy and determined souls.

CONTEMPORARY ATTITUDES

This condition was obviously discouraging to church leaders. Many suggested that the day of the rural church was over, and that rural America had lost its religious significance. Accordingly, there was no longer any need for a specific rural-directed church ministry. With a "bathtub in every home and a car in every garage" rural America could go to the city for its needs, religion included.

One point used as an argument was the decline in farm population. Governmental and educational leaders made repeated reference to the decline in the number of farmers in America. However, these people tended to overlook the fact that, while folks were leaving the farm, these same folks were not all moving to the city. "Rural population in the United States steadily increased from 1790 until 1940. . . . In 1910 there were thirty-one million farm people. This number remained almost constant until 1940. . . . In 1956 only twenty million were estimated to be on the farm." However, "the rural nonfarm population grew from eighteen million in 1910 to twenty-nine million in 1950."[4]

If we include in these statistics the number of people living in small towns we come up with a more arresting figure. According to the 1970 census, one-third of the total population of the United States, or about 60 million people, can be found in the small town and rural communities. Of this number, 22 million are unreached by the church.[5]

This, it appears, would be a sufficiently loud call for an aggressive evangelistic program in rural America. However, the scattered nature of the population, which almost precludes the building of truly large churches, and the small size of existing rural churches, has served to dampen the enthusiasm of many. Since our approaches to church ministry are geared to the larger church, the small ones continue on with little assistance. Relatively few men will give themselves to a lifetime of service in a rural church. Some seem to think that American Christianity would be better off if these smaller churches could somehow be gracefuly forgotten. One church leader suggested that, since three congregations in his area had failed to show a profit financially, they ought to be disbanded. His suggestion was accepted and the action taken.

Others have not gone quite as far. Nursing a desire to do at least something for these rural churches, many have suggested that they merge with others. One university professor has argued that all churches with less than 300 members should merge with others of the same size.[6]

Efforts in this direction have met with little success. Merger may indeed be the proper course of action in some cases, but if this is urged merely because of size, without consideration for other important factors, the move will likely be unsuccessful. We can centralize our public schools and our business if we like, for in the former case we can compel it and in the latter the medium of exchange forces people to disregard all other considerations. However, *we can never successfully centralize our churches*. At least we cannot do so and remain true to our commission. To go in this direction is to violate the very idea and genius of the church. The church was not meant to be a repository but a dispensary. She is not to conserve but to diffuse. We are not to unify, but in the good sense, to divide. Rather than aim at bringing the people to the church, the church must be taken to the people. An illustration of contemporary thinking is found in a recent publication dedicated to the building of new churches.

> It is not an entirely undesirable condition that thousands of our open country and village churches have been closed. There are declining populations in most rural communities. Improved transportation makes it possible for rural people to travel fifteen or more miles to church in less time than it takes many city people to go by bus or automobile to their churches. A general centralization of rural institutions in the larger villages and towns appears to be taking place today. It is only sensible to use the material things God has entrusted to us in the most efficient way. Instead of continuing to support small rural churches with missionary funds and part-time pastors who can provide only the most meager services for their people, we will do well wherever it is possible to merge these small churches into larger units which can carry on the work of Christ in a more effective and less costly way.[7]

It appears that the writer just quoted is gravely unfamiliar with realities of rural life. His suggestions sound theoretically plausible; and, if the policies of the church are to be patterned after those of business and education, we might try to follow his suggestions. But they are scripturally suspect and practically unsound.

An illustration will indicate the impracticability of this proposal. Imagine a small town with a population of 200 and a church with perhaps fifty people in regular attendance. We will assume that this little church decides to close for the purpose of merging with another church ten or twenty miles

distant. If half of these fifty people should drive regularly
to the next town, it would be surprising. But what shall be
done about the ones remaining? They have little spiritual
concern and consequently they will not drive these extra
miles to the house of God. And what about the children who
will grow up, marry, enter business, raise their families, grow
old, and die without a nearby testimony of the gospel?

Furthermore, what of the stabilizing influence of the local
church on the community? Communities as such are not
"saved." But a live spiritual fellowship within a community
is surely a force for righteousness. The community which is
deprived of a local church will be minus this important ingredient.

Some rural churches should indeed be closed. In certain
cases there is a rather sizeable population trend toward the
city. In some communities, churches have been built too close
together with the result that none have been able to grow.
However, this is not general, and certainly these are not the
types of communities we are concerned with at the moment.
We speak for those communities where no gospel is preached.
There are localities in our own country that are just as essentially unevangelized as many in some foreign countries.
The people do not know the gospel, have never heard a true
testimony from God, and could not make an intelligent de-
cision for or against Jesus Christ. People such as these will
likely not be reached if we follow a course of church merger.

The reasoning behind the suggestion that we should centralize our church activity is based on the fact that some
smaller churches are unable to be fully self-supporting. It is
argued that a church which cannot meet all local expenses,
plus full support for its pastor, is failing and has no right to
function.

But here some pointed questions arise. Who says so? On
what basis? Where do we find scriptural reason for believing

that a church may not function as a church just because it cannot conform to the financial requirements of our present culture? Who is to criticize a pastor for working part-time at some secular occupation in order to perform a much-needed ministry?

The Word of God teaches the support of the Christian ministry. There is no disagreement here. If the church is able to do so, there is no excuse for requiring the pastor to work at some outside employment. But it does appear that the Scriptures hold this up as a *goal* to be attained, not as a *rule* which cannot be broken. Paul taught this truth as staunchly as any, but it was not beneath his dignity to labor with his hands for two years at Corinth while establishing the young church.

And yet, many ministerial candidates are more concerned with monetary considerations than opportunities for service. It appears that we have so professionalized the Christian ministry that some of our college and seminary graduates consider it beneath their dignity to stoop to ordinary manual labor.

THE CHALLENGE

But how different from this attitude are the words of Christ when He said, "He that is greatest among you shall be your servant" (Mt 23:11). How can we reconcile present-day concepts of the Christian ministry with the life and ministry of the apostles, reformers, and martyrs who, rather than stand behind a barricade of ministerial privileges, were the first ones of the flock to suffer persecution! What right have we to claim "ministerial privileges" just because of our office?

Thank God for those sacrificing saints whose names have been emblazoned in history because of their selfless dedication. Francis Asbury, Methodist leader in America said: "My brethren seem unwilling to leave the cities, but I think I will show them the way."[8] This he did, and spent the remaining forty years of his life in strenuous missionary service.

William Warren Sweet writes as follows: "The most important single factor in Baptist expansion west of the Alleghenies and south of the Ohio . . . was the Baptist farmer-preacher. . . . The Baptist preachers lived and worked exactly as their flocks. . . . They cleared the ground, split rails, planted corn, and raised hogs on equal terms with their parishioners."[9]

We do not suggest that every pastor is to engage in manual labor. The culture of the day, not to speak of the testimony of the Word of God, demands that where possible the local church support the pastor on an economic level that will make it possible for him to put full time into his ministry. However, we do plead for the same burden for preachers of today as moved these men in their day. In America's small towns and rural areas, there is still need for those who are prepared to take the gospel at whatever personal cost, by whatever possible means, and thus to form a local fellowship of believers that will stand as a permanent witness to God and His grace.

3

The Rural Pastor

THE PASTOR OF THE TOWN and country church must possess, either by normal personality arrangement or by training, a particular philosophy of service if he is to be successful and content. This ought not to seem strange since the same thing is true for other types of service. The foreign missionary must not enter his work with the same ideas as the pastor of a large city church in the homeland. Likewise, the rural pastor must realize that everything connected with his work will be unique—the nature of it, the response to it, the number of individuals reached, and the type of approach required. If he does not reckon with these factors, and bring himself into a basic agreement with them, the odds are that he will fail.

Many rural pastorates fail because the pastor simply superimposes a city church program on a rural field. But due to the nature of the rural community, the particular scope of the rural ministry, and the specific needs encountered in such a work, it is essential that the philosophy and program of the pastor be tailored to fit his task.

Now, what are the necessary elements of this distinctive approach? Let me suggest a few thoughts for your consideration. If the rural pastor is to experience a long and contented ministry, he must have a proper concept of his work—economically, socially, and spiritually.

THE QUESTION OF MONEY

The rural pastor must settle the essential question of finances. While there may be infrequent occasions when he enjoys above average financial support, it will be seldom indeed. He will usually be supported on a lower economic standard than his city colleagues. This is perhaps one of the most pressing reasons for the difficulties facing the smaller church today. It must not be lightly dismissed. Many pastors of smaller churches find it necessary to work at some secular occupation to supplement the support they receive. Others are on a missionary basis, supported by churches or individuals who are interested in their ministry. In either of these situations, the per annum income is relatively low and perhaps inadequate. But even in those communities where the pastor is fully supported, the economic level will average considerably lower than that of the pastor of an urban church.

The pastor must be fully aware of this fact before undertaking his work. This itself will be a big step toward success. If he begins his ministry realistically, aware of the fact that he will likely meet with financial difficulties, that there will be times of economic stringency, he is less likely to be discouraged when these circumstances arise, and will be in a far better emotional state to deal with them. If he does not face this possibility before beginning his work, it is likely that some such difficulty will force him into another kind of work.

The promises of God are further encouragement. "Seek ye first the kingdom of God, and his righteousness; and all these things shall be added unto you" (Mt 6:33). And again, "But my God shall supply all your need according to his riches in glory by Christ Jesus" (Phil 4:19). God is still faithful and His promises are still true. We who have gone through financially difficult times, as we look back across the years of our ministry, can testify to the goodness of God's provision. He has proved to us as He has to others that the life of faith and dependence upon Him is sufficient.

THE PROBLEM OF SOCIAL PRESTIGE

The rural pastor must be willing to serve in a small place as long as it is God's will for him to be there. Here we go beyond the issue of economics and into the realm of social prestige and position. The twentieth century has evolved a simple method of evaluating a given ministry. If it is big, it is good! If it is small, it is of little value!

Of course, this thinking has crept into the church and has left its imprint on many young men and women. How often it has been said, "There is a young man who is destined for something big." And why? Because he is talented, intelligent, and aggressive. This idea then germinates in the mind of the prospective minister, with the result that he refuses to consider a field of service unless it is "big." Having been subjected to this reasoning through his early years it is almost impossible to change his thinking later on. Consequently, we have too many men entering the ministry who pass up opportunities for effective Christian service because they consider themselves fitted for something "bigger."

But it is interesting to observe that God does not work on this premise. Caleb, for example, exhibits every desirable trait for leadership. There is not one visible blight on his qualifications. He was faithful, dependable, imaginative, and consistent. He might easily have been leader of Israel instead of Joshua. Then why was he not? Because God chose otherwise! And there is no trace of rebellion as a result.

Consider Barnabas. Again we have a man who for sheer bigness of soul takes second place to no one. Yet he plays second fiddle to Paul. Why? Because God in His infinite wisdom planned it so.

God is not obligated to use "talent." It is true that when God does put a man in a position of leadership there is generally good reason for it, but we have no scriptural right to expect God to be overawed by great talent.

But the attitude persists, and because of it the small church is looked upon as a stepping-stone to something bigger, and service accepted in its behalf is usually viewed as a temporary and unimportant interlude.

But right at this point it is essential that we think *sensibly* and *scripturally*. Bigness for the sake of bigness alone leaves much to be desired. Seeking a big church simply for the prestige and position one gains socially is hardly consistent with the calling of a minister. In fact, even the contention that one is seeking a larger place *in order to reach more people* in itself can be a most unworthy motive.

There is serious doubt, both scripturally and logically, about our present-day ideas of church life and growth. The larger a church becomes the more impersonal it becomes. An individual is often lost in the crowd. The idea of fellowship, so prominent in the early church, is often inadequately experienced in a truly large church. The organization tends to become "institutionalized" instead of "individualized."

"As churches grow big, they become impersonal. . . . It seems as though the larger they have grown, the further they have drifted from the basic starting point in Christian life and teachings. The reasoning seems to be something like this: Bigness is an indication of greatness; greatness is an indication of success; therefore, success must be judged in size. Is this basic? Is it Christian?"[1]

The country church pastor must settle once for all the question of his life purpose. Carl Clark has summed it up this way: "Will he set himself to climb the ladder of so-called pastoral success? Is he ambitious to try to push himself into high denominational positions and widespread influence?

Or is his primary purpose to serve wherever the place of service may be most effective? . . . Once this purpose has been set, he is not quite so anxious to get a new church as he is to make a better church of the one he has. Once he has this dedication, he is more concerned with the investment of his life than he is with the attainment of success."[2]

Of course there are discouragements in the rural pastorate. There are seemingly insurmountable obstacles that equal and in some cases surpass those faced by the urban pastor. It is therefore absolutely essential that the pastor face the call to the smaller church as clearly as any worker faces the call to any other ministry. Clark comments, "He must have a heart so firmly set on his task that neither doubt nor trouble, disappointment nor temptation can turn him aside. With this motive he can persist. Without it he will probably move."[3]

THE FOCUS OF SPIRITUAL IMPACT

The rural pastor must not only see the fallacy of seeking a large place of service for itself alone, but he must recognize the importance of service in a small-town situation. It will be seen that this ministry differs in scope, numbers, nature, and results. These differences must be recognized and clearly understood if one is to experience satisfaction.

The small town and rural ministry differs from the city ministry in *scope*. It is doubtful that the rural pastor will exercise a great amount of influence outside his own community. Due to the closely knit community life and the exclusive spirit sometimes found in rural areas, the pastor will experience his greatest satisfaction in ministering to his own community—to people he knows by first names, to those whose problems and successes are intimately known to him and with whom he has counselled and worked. In fact, until he arrives at this place of intimacy, his ministry will be ineffective.

On the contrary, the scope of the city pastorate may reach

into many separate communities. This is occasioned by the fact that the average city church draws its constituents from outside its immediate locality. The members come from all over the city and surrounding towns as well; therefore the community aspects of the pastorate of the city church will not be so prominent.

City and rural pastorates also differ in the *numbers reached*. The city pastor will doubtless speak on the average to a greater number of people than the village minister. But if this is true, it is no less true that the ministries differ just as widely in *nature,* and here the smaller pastorate more than compensates for the fewer number of individuals.

It is a fact easily proved that one man can only minister personally and individually to a specific number of individuals. I am not concerned here with the number, for there would be no unanimity of opinion. However, no one will dispute the simple fact itself. One man is only one, and there are only twenty-four hours in a day, only seven days a week. When this time is used, there is no more, and there is certainly a limit as to the number of people to whom any person can effectively minister in this period of time. When the number grows beyond this hypothetical point, it becomes necessary to utilize a variety of associates. When this happens, the personal ministry of the pastor to the individual is sharply curtailed. He becomes primarily an administrator. The personal relationship is then almost certain to be delegated to others, a circumstance that is never wholly satisfactory.

On the contrary, it is seldom that a village pastorate will grow beyond the ability of one man to know intimately and well each and every member of his church. Carl Clark has well spoken of this as a "depth ministry" contrasted to "breadth ministry."[4] Thus, while not reaching the masses, the rural pastor can rejoice that he is reaching the few with an impact that would be virtually impossible in the larger church. This is the difference in *nature* between service in the small rural church and the larger city church.

The elements that go into the building of character come by close and intimate contact. "Many things in life can be passed on by mass communication techniques. News, information, and ideas spread very quickly and to large numbers of people through modern means of mass communication. These facilities have given marvelous opportunities for spreading of the ideas of the Gospel. Such means as the printed page and modern radio and television are cases in point. By these means one person can give an idea to several million people at one time."[5]

However, Clark continues, "The more vital things of Christianity and the more essential qualities of character development . . . are not communicated this way. . . . As a rule, . . . character is built through intimate relations in repeated occurrences. Character is not built in a moment. Character is the process of maturing an individual's life over an extended time."[6]

This is ministry in depth, and is the unquestioned opportunity of the small town minister. Not for a moment would we imply that the city pastor is deprived of the same opportunity. But we unhesitatingly affirm that the man who lives, works, and serves in a rural community, who prays with, counsels with, preaches to the people of that community, has a distinct advantage.

Finally, the two ministries differ in *results*. Rather than building a bigger and bigger church, the rural minister makes his greatest impact on people over a long period of time. He has an opportunity of actually helping to direct community life. No community will ever be totally "christianized," but surely the minister who will faithfully preach the message of God will leave the imprint of his ministry upon community life. It cannot be otherwise.

The village pastor has an opportunity to lead young folks. Rural areas are teeming with youth. It is the soul-satisfying privilege of the rural minister to evangelize and nurture these young lives into pathways of fruitful service. What greater legacy could one leave than a score or more of young people who have been regenerated, trained, and sent out into Christian service? What more lasting results could one ask from his life and ministry?

What is your philosophy of Christian service? I urge you to give serious thought to the matter. Something of the ideas embodied in this chapter must be realized in the heart and soul of the minister of the gospel if he would serve successfully in the small-town church.

4

A Church Is Born

A PROSPEROUS, THRIVING CHURCH is not an accident. It is almost always true that a growing, spiritual, soul-winning church can trace its history to the ministry of some wise servant of God who followed sound principles in its beginning. These principles must be stated and studied!

Our major purpose in this chapter will be to identify the initial steps involved in beginning a new ministry in a churchless area.

CHOOSING AND ENTERING YOUR FIELD OF SERVICE

Every town needs the witness of a local fellowship of believers. But we must face the fact that this ideal will never be fully realized. In some areas it will be impossible to establish a local church. Where this is the case some other method must be used to reach the people. However, this is not our concern at the moment. The question is How shall we choose the community in which a church can be established?

CONSIDER ALL THE FACTORS WHEN DECIDING ON YOUR FIELD

Size is one such factor! A Christian worker should hardly consider spending his full time ministering in an area with a population of only twenty-five people. It would seem that a prospective area should have a population of perhaps 150 people in addition to surrounding areas. The smaller communities are just as needy and certainly dare not be neglected but can perhaps be reached with a weekly Bible class as a local church outreach.

The size of the community must then be weighed alongside other circumstances, such as the nearest other community, nearest church, and so on. Common courtesy, not to speak of Christian ethics, demand that we honor another servant of Christ who may be preaching the gospel nearby even though we may not agree with him on some minor points of doctrine.

Have you any means of contact with the people? This may be a determining consideration. If we are faced with two openings, not knowing which to enter, we would probably be wise, all other things being equal, to enter the one with which some contact has been established. Sometimes a friend or relative can help acquaint us with a needy area, or an individual in one community may have friends in a more distant place where spiritual need exists.

Some have hesitated to enter certain communities because of their reputation for wickedness. But this attitude scarcely seems compatible with Scripture. If we have the answer to man's sin, then the darkest places need it the most. If a foreign missionary feels impelled to enter the darkest areas of heathen immorality, shall we refrain from taking the gospel of Christ to equally needy communities at home?

The most important consideration in choosing your field is the leading of the Lord. The Holy Spirit knows exactly what our capabilities are, in which location we are best fitted to serve, and what community most needs our special contribution. Therefore, seek the mind of the Lord above everything else.

BEGIN WITH A HEALTHY ATTITUDE

The work must be begun optimistically, with a deep-seated assurance that God has directed us, and that in God's own time and way His blessing will be experienced.

This spiritual optimism is vital, for there are many circumstances that will drain our supply to the last drop. Chief among these is the "wait and see" attitude so often encountered. This is disconcerting, especially if we have assumed that unsaved people are pining in spiritual sorrow, waiting for a preacher to give them the gospel.

Another disturbing element is the lack of appreciation for our service. We may help clothe the naked, feed the hungry, attend the sick, bury the dead, rebuke the sinner, instruct the anxious, spend hours in study and prayer, and sometimes work additional hours at secular employment. It is only human to expect some word of thanks from those we serve. But it will frequently be forgotten! While a few discerning souls will express their gratefulness occasionally, most will accept our ministries without saying "thanks."

This should not seem strange. There were ten lepers cleansed by our Lord and only one returned to thank Him. Our experience will be the same. Remember that we are serving our Lord Jesus first of all. It is true that we give our lives to others, but unless they are given first to Christ, our giving to others will be weighed in the balance of how much we receive in return.

LIVE IN THE COMMUNITY YOU PLAN TO SERVE

Your ministry will be more effective if you live in the area in which you work. Small-town people are social people and will be drawn to the person who honestly seeks to be one of them. The faith we profess and preach must be lived before the people we serve. More desirable accommodations could possibly be found in large cities, but you would then miss out on community contacts.

GET ACQUAINTED WITH YOUR PEOPLE

Regardless of what official contacts have been made by the

organization with which you are associated, you should make it your business to visit in every home as soon as possible. There is usually an unseen wall of resistance to a new minister and this must somehow be broken down. House-to-house calls will serve the purpose better than anything else. It may be helpful to compile a simple questionnaire, asking just the names, address, number in family, and church affiliation of the people. This would enable the minister to make his calls with a bit less stiffness. Whatever method is used, personal, friendly, immediate contact is necessary.

The First Beginnings of the Work

Begin a week-night bible class

The usual approach is to start with a Sunday school, then proceed to a full program as rapidly as possible. However, there are some good reasons for believing that a week-night Bible class, either in a home or some other central location, serves the purpose better than a Sunday school. This is not to underestimate the value of the Sunday school as a ministry in its own right. However, it has lost some effectiveness as a means of starting a church. Therefore, we strongly urge the use of the week-night Bible class. Note some of its advantages.

1. It does not promise as much as a Sunday school, therefore a week-night Bible class can be begun and later dropped, if it does not prove successful, without much ill-effect.
2. If a Bible class does grow, it will form the best possible base upon which to build a permanent work.
3. A Bible class usually solves the problem of a meeting place. It can often be held in homes.
4. A week-night Bible class will more likely reach the unsaved men in the community than will a Sunday school, which has been typed in the minds of many as a service for old people, women, and children. Those men, however,

who disdain the Sunday school can often be reached in their own homes by the week-night Bible class.

5. People will be saved through this ministry.
6. The week-night Bible class provides a way whereby the minister can easily broaden his work to other areas. Even though a minister is occupied fully each Lord's Day in his own work, there will be some communities close by in which a mid-week service can be held. By conducting a Bible class there he may be instrumental in helping to start another full-time church.

A few facts concerning the Bible class must be kept in mind. Keep your messages simple and informal. Do not conduct your services as you would a formal service in a church. Keep your Bible study basic and foundational. Emphasize the great fundamental doctrines of the Word of God. Teach clearly the plan of salvation and Paul's epistles as they relate to personal Christian conduct and the building of the local church. Strive above all else to communicate God's message clearly to your hearers.

USE THE SUNDAY SCHOOL

The Sunday school is an excellent companion ministry to the Bible class. Sometimes it may be scheduled to run parallel with the weekly Bible class. At other times it may be organized only after the Bible class has provided a good base for more permanent work. In any event, those who are reached for Christ can be instructed in a properly directed Sunday school while unsaved can be reached for Christ.

In the beginning of your work, you may have to get along with a skeleton teaching force and just a few classes. Do not let this discourage you. It is not necessary to have your school fully graded and departmentalized in order to be effective. Flannelgraph material and other teaching aids which will offset these handicaps can be used.

DEVELOP A YOUTH PROGRAM

Most smaller communities have a large number of young folks, many of whom will not attend the services at the church. A live, aggressive youth program will help reach them. This youth service should perhaps be scheduled on a weekly basis, and for the best results should be planned for home or some other neutral place. The emphasis should be on fellowship, recreation, and study. These youth meetings ought not be duplicates of the regular church services, but should be aimed directly at the young person. No regular preaching should be done, though a devotional time is essential.

PLAN A DAILY VACATION BIBLE SCHOOL

A daily vacation Bible school, aside from being an excellent evangelistic tool, makes possible a wide contact with the families in the community. Parents have frequently begun regular church attendance after coming to the closing program of a well-conducted daily vacation Bible school.

INVESTIGATE WAYS OF ENLARGING YOUR MINISTRY

Local regulations vary greatly, and what is acceptable in some is unacceptable in others. However, in some instances you will find it possible to go into the local school with some type of Bible-teaching program. It may be released time or, as is the case in certain areas, a Bible club may be conducted immediately after school hours in a nearby home. Aside from this, there are other avenues of service available through various child evangelism organizations and youth-oriented organizations. In whatever way possible, seek to be used of God to make His Word known to every person in your community.

THREE TYPES OF COMMUNITIES

THE CLOSED-CHURCH COMMUNITY

The average closed-church community will contain the following ingredients: a usable building, several hundred spiritually needy and forgotten individuals, a general unconcern about spiritual truth, and perhaps one or two persons who recall the blessings of former days and almost with despair keep trusting that the former glory will be restored. It is the task of the rural pastor to enter this field and so mix these ingredients together that out of them will come a stable, self-governing, self-supporting church.

It must be borne in mind that at one time the church was active—the center of a live spiritual program which brought great blessing to the community. Now that interest is gone! It will be the work of the new minister to make this church again a blessing and bring these people to the place where they realize that a progressive spiritual church is a necessity in their community.

This will mean that a revival message must be preached. Christians will have to have their "pure minds" stirred up by the way of remembrance. Sin must be uncovered and dealt with. The message of the Word of God must be applied to wrong attitudes, inconsistent Christian living, and carelessness. The great doctrines of the Word must be preached. Most people in such communities, even those who are believers, have been so long without a faithful witness that their hearts are calloused and cold. The truth they once knew is perhaps forgotten or tragically dimmed. Therefore, it is necessary to remind them again of the great salvation truths of John, Romans, and Galatians; the practical truth of 1 and 2 Corinthians, Philippians, and Colossians; and the church truth of Paul's epistle to the Ephesians. All this must form the structure of real, solid, revival preaching. Apart from such a scriptural foundation, appeals to higher Christian living will be only temporarily effective, if at all.

The program of the reopened church will have to be advertised. There are effective ways to do this:

1. Plan special services with a good, interesting speaker who is in sympathy with your work. Make sure every person in the community knows of the services. Print or mimeograph announcements and distribute them from door to door.
2. Send out weekly or monthly bulletins to all the residents in the neighborhood. Give your publication a name, include a short devotional, publish items of community interest, and publicize your church schedule.
3. Plan for a closing program in your daily vacation Bible school and special programs at Easter and Christmas and invite all the community residents for the services.
4. Engage in regular weekly visitation. Visit and revisit every home. Continual friendly contact is invaluable in the progress of the work. In these visits it is not always necessary to preach to the people. Make friends with them, then the task of leading them to Christ will be considerably easier.

If the people have not moved away from the closed church such a program will, with prayer and dependence upon God, bring results. And this latter must not be ignored. "Prayer changes things" is more than a nice-sounding phrase for a motto on the wall. It is a statement of spiritual reality. Then pray! When the way looks blackest and the possibility of victory seems most remote—PRAY! God does hear and answer.

THE UNCHURCHED COMMUNITY

Here you will find much the same condition as that of the closed-church community but with a few differences. In the first place you will not have even a fabric of church loyalty to work with. Since most of the residents come from irreligious backgrounds, common church practices such as giving and regular church attendance are completely unknown.

Another difference, on the positive side, is more encouraging. There are generally no old church feuds to contend with. Some closed churches have church skeletons in the closet, and when the church is opened again old grudges and feuds are resurrected.

Again, there are not so many wrong ideas to be set right. It is actually more difficult to teach one who has been mistaught, than to teach the person who is completely ignorant. Since most of the folks in an unchurched area fit into this category, the minister will find it easier to instruct his hearers in the truth of the Word of God.

One problem encountered in the unchurched community is that of a suitable building. Sometimes it may be necessary to use a community hall or school. One group used an old, abandoned house. It was unfit to live in and part of the porch was unsafe, but it served the purpose at least temporarily. This same group later met in the open under a huge oak tree. Electric lights were strung up, old church benches borrowed, a platform erected, and a pulpit built.

The importance of personal friendly contact in a new work cannot be overemphasized. In all probability the new minister will be an outsider who is not known to the people. They are unacquainted with his family background, his personal convictions, and his personality. They are not sure he will fit into their social pattern. Consequently they will withhold approval until he proves himself. To enjoy the hand of friendship, one must merit it. There is no shortcut to this goal. It may take a long time—a year, two years, or even longer—but it is worth it. Without this asset your preaching will do very little good; therefore, get close to the people. Visit them in their homes. Serve them when they are ill and minister to them when in spiritual need. This is the pathway to community acceptance. If this sounds strange or impossible, then perhaps you need to rethink your call to the town or country church.

THE COMMUNITY WITH THE INEFFECTIVE CHURCH

The spiritual needs of a community with an ineffective church are more difficult to meet than either of the other two. However, if the gospel is not being preached, the spiritual need is just as great as anywhere else; and our Lord is certainly just as concerned that this need be met.

Perhaps the only possible course of action here is organization of a Bible class. In beginning such a class, no mention would be made of starting a church. The aim is to get God's Word to the people. If this results in revival in the present church, then you have accomplished your purpose. However, if it only brings opposition on the part of the leaders while hearts continue to be blessed by the Holy Spirit, then it will likely lead on to the formation of a permanent work.

We must urge here the guidance of the Holy Spirit. In this condition more than in any other, the Christian worker exposes himself to great danger. Satan will take every opportunity to gain an advantage. Men are never so aroused as when organized religion is opposed, though it be ever so dead and lifeless. Let us therefore be Christian gentlemen in whatever we do.

CONCLUDING NOTES

MEET THE NEED OF ALL AGE GROUPS

Our major efforts should be directed toward the establishment of the local church. This means that the adults of the community must be reached in order that they may in God's time shoulder the responsibilities of the work. But while we concern ourselves with the parents, let us not forget the children. We cannot build a church without adults, but we will not have a future church if we neglect the young folks.

MAKE THE CHURCH THE CENTER OF COMMUNITY LIFE

A generation ago the village church was the center of social as well as religious life. In our day the center has shifted from the church to the school. In short, we have exchanged the gospel for education, and we are suffering because of it. Let us resolve therefore to make our church fellowship a thing of blessing and beauty, not only on the Lord's Day but through the week as well. This is difficult but not impossible.

KEEP AT YOUR WORK

Someone has coined the word *unstoppable* in describing the proper attitude of the servant of Christ. This is an apt term. As long as the Lord has not definitely led you away from the field, then remain there. And let us guard against using human inclinations as the leadings of the Holy Spirit. The devil would like nothing better than to remove a pastor *just before the moment of victory.*

KEEP THE WORD OF GOD PREEMINENT

This should be obvious but it is too important to take for granted. The Word of God given in the power of the Holy Spirit is the thing God promises to bless. Whether in children's work, youth work, or preaching ministry, let us *give the Word.* No clever schemes, elaborate programs, or gimmicks can in themselves be a blessing. We must give forth the Word of life which is itself life-giving.

5

Church Organization

Every church ought to be organized, yet it is astonishing how many churches are either *not* organized, or organized improperly. One soon discovers, of course, that there are rather strong reasons why some people object to organization. Some have been in groups that were saddled with an unwieldy constitution. In other cases some religious "dictator" in the name of "organization" has ruled with an iron hand. Others hold to their opposition because of invalid but preconceived ideas. For these and other reasons many possess a deep-seated distrust of organizational operation.

Perhaps at this point it might be well to define organization. Webster says the word *organize* means "to arrange or form into a coherent unity or functioning whole; to set up an administrative structure for; . . . to arrange by systematic planning and united effort." To put this into another form, we might say simply that proper organization is that orderly outline of procedures by which the aim and goal of the group is clarified and most quickly and effectively reached. It can safely be said that any organization which does not fit into this definition cannot be good organization.

There are some definite benefits connected with good organization, among them the following:

1. The aim and purpose of the group is clarified.

2. Efficiency is encouraged. Overlapping of responsibility and wasted motion is evident in unorganized groups. Certain individuals have more responsibility than they deserve. Others perhaps more capable have little or none. Only by sensible organization will a group be able to function efficiently.

3. Unity is maintained. Churches and religious groups torn by strife and dissension are many times suffering from the consequences of poor organization.

4. The group is protected. Many unorganized churches have suffered serious deterioration, sometimes having been scattered or assimilated by some other group. Those who were saved will be an eternal tribute to the labor of the servant of the Lord, but no lasting ministry has resulted.

5. The well-organized group is respected. Careful handling of funds, proper records, sound management, all tend to command the respect of those within the church, and what is more important, those outside whom we are trying to reach. It seems senseless to be so concerned that our secular businesses are carefully administered while the Lord's work, which is many times more important, is carried on in a slipshod fashion.

The first step one could take in eliminating objection to organization might logically be an emphatic statement of its values. Point out the advantages which could be realized by adopting a constitution. If this work is done well by the pastor, it may be found that people will cooperate much more quickly than imagined.

However, some exceptional cases may persist. A few individuals may continue to oppose organization. In order to assist the Christian worker in every way possible, we offer the following suggestions for leading a group of Christians in the task of organization:

1. Do not question the motives of the one who is unable to see eye-to-eye with you. Very possibly he is not as stubborn as he first appears to be.

2. Do not endeavor to win your point by mere argument. Discussion is necessary, but beware of pushing the matter to the point where the other person must "fight" or "lose face." Keep the discussion on such a level that the other individual is able to maintain his personal dignity.

3. Do not seek to rally enough support for your point of view to "smother" the other fellow. This usually results in defeat instead of victory.

4. Do not forget that the other person is an individual. Treat him as you wish to be treated. Sit where he sits! Imagine yourself in the minority and act accordingly.

5. Do not confuse essentials with nonessentials. More than one Christian leader has won an insignificant victory while losing a worthwhile war. In any task of organization there are certain points which can be bypassed easily enough with no harm to the finished product. Take care that you contend for the points that are most important.

6. Do not speak until you know what you are going to say. It is unlikely that you will gain much support if you do not understand the facts yourself. Take time to study the issues carefully before proposing.

7. Do not rush. Take plenty of time. Do not run ahead of your people. In the work of organization we must bring our people with us every step of the way. It matters little if your goal is postponed a month, six months, or even a year. Better to arrive then as a unit than to arrive earlier divided into splinter groups.

8. Finally, don't give up! In the great majority of instances, the pastor can have what he sincerely believes will benefit the group provided he follows these suggestions. In almost every case, opposition can be overcome. It is possible

to do God's work in a spirit of love and consideration, without excruciating clashes of personalities and programs.

How soon should organization take place? The answer depends on how the church was begun and its subsequent rate of growth. For example, in one community a denomination may find a nucleus of people whose convictions or past associations make them good prospects as future members. After counsel and preliminary planning the church may decide to organize a local fellowship there. In such a case there may be a sufficient number of qualified men available immediately to organize the church. If this is the situation, then it may be that if organization were long delayed the work would suffer because of it. On the other hand, the same conditions may exist except that there are not enough men in the group who are prepared to accept responsibility. In this case organization ought certainly to be delayed until such a time as there are local Christians available to serve as leaders in the group. If there are not enough individuals available, or if those who are available are not qualified, it is too soon for organization.

Another case may be noted. In this community we will suppose that a number of Christians are concerned that there is no sound gospel church within driving distance. These Christians themselves band together, form a simple organization, perhaps even elect church officers, and call a pastor. In this case also it is quite possible that immediate organization is proper and advantageous for the group.

However, the condition which expressly concerns us is somewhat different. I am thinking now of the pastor who goes into a spiritually needy community—without invitation to do so, with no promise that he will receive support, and certainly with no hope that there are any persons who can be immediately counted upon for leadership. He may begin the ministry on the general principles outlined in the beginning of this book and eventually, under the blessing of the Lord, witness the salvation of a number of souls, their growth in grace, and their desire for a local fellowship. This process may take six months, a year, or even longer. The question is, "When shall such a work be organized?"

While I do not think it is possible to set any time limit that will be valid in all cases, it is possible to list certain guides that will pinpoint the proper time for organizaiton.

1. Do not organize until there have been a dozen or two local individuals converted and established in the faith. These ought to be persons who are stable, community citizens, people of reasonably long residence in the area.

2. Do not organize until at least three men have been converted who possess leadership ability, who are established in the faith, and sufficiently respected in the community to bear some responsibility.

3. Do not organize until the group is sufficiently mature to do some constructive thinking about organization.

Now then, how does one go about beginning the work of organization? First, let the pastor acquire as many constitutions from other churches as possible. Get a half dozen or more from churches both large and small. Then—study them. Note wherein they agree and wherein they differ and seek to find out why. Acquaint yourself with constitutional "language."

Following this, draw up a suggested constitution and by-laws for your own group. Abstract from these sample constitutions the things that are particularly fitted for your situation. Remember that the constitution of any group is simply *an instrument to guide the group in the work it is set up to perform.* It stands to reason that the task of your group is not identical with that of others so your constitution will also differ from theirs.

Now, after drawing up a proposed constitution, carefully edit it. Spend much time on it. Lay it aside and forget it for a week or two. Compare it again with your group and see how well it fits. Where something unnecessary or superfluous has crept in, remove it. Where something has been forgotten, insert it. Rework it and rework it again.

At this point you are ready to work with several others on a constitution committee. It may be that the fellowship has within it several men recognized as leaders. These could be invited to assist in such work. Or perhaps the church would vote for a three-man committee to work with the pastor. In one way or another, bring a small group together for the purpose of writing a constitution for your church.

The pastor then may meet with this committee and tell them of his hopes for a constitution. At this time he will introduce them to his own work and present to them his *proposed constitution*. Do not forget that it is still just that, insofar as the group is concerned. Regardless how much work he may have put in it, it is still only a personal proposal and must be considered as such.

This committee then proceeds to go over the proposal, and after they have completed their work, the constitution will be presented to the church as a *proposal from the committee*. From this point, it is usually not difficult to bring the process to a successful conclusion. Each point should be read and voted upon separately, and the final constitution then adopted. At this point, the task is completed and the group is in possession of a constitution which will serve to guide it through the future. Through wise leadership, cooperation, and persistence, a church can thus evolve a method of self-government. It can be an important milestone in its history.

6

Confronting Organizational Issues

THE TASK OF CHURCH ORGANIZATION can pose a variety of problems. In this chapter we survey some of these problems and attempt to find some answers for them.

INTERIM ORGANIZATION

This phrase describes the elementary organization which may be necessary in a new work before it is advanced far enough to accept full self-government.

Since many small town pastors deal with those who have little or no background in church life, it is not only necessary to bring them to Christ but to establish them in the faith and instruct them in their proper discharge of church responsibilities. During this period of development, there often will be found impelling reasons why some type of temporary organization is necessary. The people themselves may desire it, or some outside circumstance may require that the young church be protected.

The question then is this: If the group is not ready for full organization, what other course of action may be taken? In some cases a parent church may sponsor a new fellowship and then proceed to carry some of the financial load, provide some of the work force, and may even retain control of church property. However, in other cases, this is not possible.

It has been the author's privilege to work with young rural

churches in these very circumstances, and to observe others who have faced similar difficulties. Out of this experience and observation a possible answer has developed.

Instead of full organization, a young church may begin with a simple doctrinal statement. This could be copied after that of some other sound evangelical group. Then all those who can give satisfactory testimony to personal salvation and are willing to agree in writing to the statement of faith could form the charter membership of the new group. This would provide a starting point. Business could be transacted, officers could be elected, and discipline could be exercised. Such action would serve to protect the group, would provide a basis of fellowship, and would, most important of all, prepare for full organization later on. As the group enlarges and becomes more stable, the full constitution could be adopted, and the statement of faith could then be incorporated into the constitution and by-laws.

This temporary or interim organization could continue indefinitely. There would be no need to rush into something for which the group is unprepared. Ample time would be given for laying the groundwork for a sound organizational superstructure.

Here again it is important that we keep in mind one essential fact, that organization is not an end in itself. It is only a tool to do a job and must therefore be kept in its place.

Premature Organization

There are those who feel that, in order to designate a certain group as a "church," it is necessary that the group have a full complement of deacons and elders, a church secretary, a Sunday school superintendent, assistant superintendent, song leader, and trustees. In other words, if we are going to call it a church, it has to meet our clearly defined pattern at all points.

This is unfortunate. There are many instances where churches today are either closed or where they remain static and ineffective because in their beginning some overzealous pastor foisted organization upon them too quickly.

We believe that a church, to grow and increase in effectiveness, ought to be organized. But while we deplore unorganized churches we equally object to premature organization. Serious consequences may result from premature organization, both to churches and individuals. The church itself may become spiritually impotent, torn by strife, division, and bickering. The effect on individuals in the church may be even more disastrous. An unstable believer in such a situation may assert himself as the indispensable person and quickly develop into a "church boss." Others may be thrust into positions of leadership for which they are unprepared and become stagnated.

Guard against premature organization. It is far better to continue with a minimum of organization a bit too long than to organize too quickly or too extensively and so do spiritual harm to immature believers.

Excessive Organization

Sometimes we encounter a situation where a constitution has been formed and adopted, but which is too complicated for the group. One pastor faced this difficulty. A previous pastor had entered the area, carried on a ministry for sometime, and just before leaving hurriedly proposed a constitution. The inexperienced group trustingly adopted it.

This was bad enough. But the complexity and size of the constitution aggravated the problem. There were not enough church members to fill all the offices which the constitution required. In addition, there was one person in the group who was determined that since this constitution was legally adopted it must be followed in every detail.

In these cases human counsel is of little value. But pastors must be aware that such problems exist. While there may be no good way of remedying this situation, we may at least make sure we do not leave such a condition for those who follow us.

Bear this fact in mind. It is not always possible to reach our ideals instantly. In some areas of our ministry we may never achieve our loftiest aims. Some perplexities and problems must be lived with for a long time. Let us trust God for clarity of vision to see our proper goals. But let us also ask Him for patience in seeking to reach them.

> Dear Lord,
> Give me courage to change the things that can be changed,
> Patience to bear the things I cannot change,
> And wisdom to know the difference.
>
> PETER MARSHALL

ORGANIZATION AND CHURCH OWNERSHIP

Church ownership is no serious problem in a new work. Usually, someone in the area will give or sell some land very cheaply and the church thus built belongs, of course, to the people who built it.

However, there are matters that even here should be carefully watched. First be sure to pay a token amount for the land. This closes the deal and removes all doubt of ownership in the future. Then, if the property is legally deeded and if some payment is made, make sure that nothing is inserted in the deed that could cause trouble later on. Some people who give property to churches attempt to include provisions in the deed that make it possible to interfere with the church at some future time. It pays to seek out reputable legal advice and make sure that you are on solid ground.

The reopened church is more likely to have property problems than a new work. Each case includes some aspects which make it unique among all others.

There are instances where church buildings, long since

empty, are owned legally and properly by some religious group. Sometimes these groups do not want them to come under control or ownership of someone else. Remember that the Christian worker must never engage in any action that could logically be construed as "church stealing."

In cases where churches have been built as community churches, (by which term we mean a church with no denominational bias, set up on an ill-defined organizational pattern, with no clearly-defined doctrinal position) one sometimes finds difficulty in leading the church on to a proper scriptural position. Many times an elementary constitution has been adopted years before and there is no interest in any amendments or revisions. In this event it may be that a solid work cannot be done and a better course of action would be to begin work somewhere else.

Another situation sometimes encountered is where no clear deed is available, or where the deed is recorded but because of careless wording is not clear in its meaning. The details can be so confusing that attorneys themselves almost despair. I know of one church which was built many years ago, the land having been deeded to a particular group in the community with the provision that the church be built with a Masonic lodge on the second floor. The Masonic lodge part was never built, but the man who deeded the building did nothing about it until almost thirty years later. Then after the ownership of the building was so much in doubt that everyone was claiming it though no one had a clear deed to it, the donor went to the one remaining officer of the church, got him to sign off, and reclaimed the property under the terms of the original agreement! He then re-sold it to the community, under the control of a group of local trustees.

Sometimes, in cases where the church is properly owned by a certain group, there will be interest in selling the property at a reasonable figure.

ORGANIZATION AND INCORPORATION

Two methods of church ownership are possible. One is to have the church owned by the trustee board, with the members elected from among the constituency. This method is used in many cases, especially in rural communities. Where it is properly controlled it is satisfactory. However, several things need to be taken into consideration.

A church organized in this way has no legal status as a group in most states. It is unable to hold real estate in its own name, cannot contract business transactions, and is not permitted to sue at law. All the business of the church must be carried on by the trustees and in their name. Money borrowed by the church must be borrowed on their signature or chattel mortgage, secured by the property of the trustees. In certain cases individual trustee members may be held responsible for outstanding bills. Furthermore, the church is not permitted to grant receipts for gifts given to it. Consequently, such gifts are not legally deductible from income-tax reports of the donors. In addition, it frequently happens that the congregation fails to elect new trustee board members, with the result that the board partially or entirely dies out, and the church is left without anyone to act on its behalf.

On the other hand, the church may organize itself as an incorporation. In this way a church is legally recognized by the state as a corporate body. "An incorporated congregation is a legal entity, a being separate from the individuals who constitute its membership. As such, it is entitled to all the rights of an individual. It can hold any property, including real estate, and go to court in its own name," explains Harold Linamen, who also points out four advantages of incorporation:

1. Individual members are not responsible for any of the acts of the corporation.

2. Trustees are not individually liable for debts or judgments against the corporation, unless they have exceeded their authority in incurring liabilities or engaging in contract.

3. Once a church has been incorporated it is not possible for another church in the same state to receive a charter employing the same name.

4. The incorporated church has continued life: it does not cease to exist upon the death of its incorporators.[1]

Contrary to popular ideas, incorporation of a local church is not an especially difficult matter. Details vary a bit from state to state, so the best course of action is to seek the counsel of an attorney. However, in most cases it is simply a matter of submitting to the secretary of state the necessary legal forms and papers. The process is quite inexpensive, even when including the services of an attorney.

A further fact about tax-deductible receipts should be clarified. It is not enough for a church to be legally incorporated. After incorporation the church must make formal request to the district director of internal revenue for tax-exempt status. Only when this is granted can tax-deductible receipts be given legally.

In closing, a few things ought to be said of a general nature. Try by all means to make contact with some reputable attorney near your field of service. There will be many problems of a local nature that will be understood by your neighborhood lawyer. He can help you around many difficult situations.

If you are faced with a problem relating to your church that involves the ownership of the building, seek out the deed and study it. All land that is legally owned has a deed recorded in the county courthouse. Find out in what section of the county the land is located. Then go to the county clerk, get the exact location of it, and find out from the abstract office the number and page in the deed record book where it can be found. These records are kept for public use. A few moments spent here will help you to move with assurance later on.

7

Planning the Church Program

FOR OUR PURPOSE, the "church program" will be divided into three parts: its meetings, its evangelistic outreach, and its finances.

THE CHURCH AND ITS MEETINGS

Most churches have what is called a full church program, which usually includes two services on Sunday, a week-night prayer or Bible study service, and a youth service. We are primarily concerned however with what these meetings accomplish than with their date on the calendar. What, really, is the purpose behind our stated services? We speak of a "full church program"; but what is this church program accomplishing? Scripturally, our public services should aim at the following: Christian fellowship, inspiration, indoctrination, and spiritual maturation.

First, consider this matter of Christian fellowship. It appears that the outstanding characteristic of the early believers was the fellowship that existed among them. "And they continued stedfastly in the apostles' doctrine and fellowship, and in breaking of bread" (Ac 2:42). Not only did the apostolic church *enjoy* fellowship; it *was* a fellowship. It scarcely needs saying that we have lost this in today's typical church and it is imperative that we rediscover it. Our church services should be an experience of fellowship of the warmest and most spiritual nature. The worship services of our churches ought not be stereotyped, lethargic gatherings which leave us cold and untouched. By the help of the Holy Spirit and by a determination to be satisfied with nothing less, we must recapture the sense of oneness that so characterized the first-century believers.

This experience of fellowship need not be restricted to the public worship services of the church. The local church which has come to know the joy of meeting informally in the homes of the members, in the village park, or at some other neutral place, joining together in testimony, prayer fellowship, and mutual edification finds that even the worship services take on new meaning. The pastor should resolve therefore to do everything possible toward making the church a true, scriptural, New Testament fellowship of Christians.

Second, the services of the church should provide inspiration for the depressed, despairing, and defeated. The average minister, looking over his flock on a Sunday morning, possibly would be distressed if he knew how many were laboring under an almost unbearable burden. For these there must be inspiration. Luke tells us that our Lord came to "preach the gospel to the poor . . . to heal the brokenhearted" (Lk 4:18). Let His ministers do likewise. May the pastor remember that he has a responsibility to "lift up the hands which hang down" (Heb 12:12). Our people need inspiration.

Third, we must indoctrinate our people. They must be instructed in the Word of God. The members of our congregation should learn something through our teaching and preaching. The elements of the Christian faith must be inculcated into their hearts and lives. People who listen to our sermons should be able to give an answer to those who ask them of the hope that is within them.

It is tragic but true, however, that this has not generally been the result of our preaching. Our pulpits have become famous for almost everything except biblical instruction. Superficial sermonizing has taken the place of solid scriptural exposition. The suppositions of modern science and education have usurped the "thus saith the Lord." As a result we have on our hands a generation of untaught Christians, espousing a cause they are unable to define, supporting a movement they do not understand. Many Christians have wasted countless man-hours listening to moral lectures or semi-scriptural sermonettes which have totally failed to do what a sermon ought to do—instruct!

This is not to deny that sermons must do more than instruct. There are times when the pastor must rebuke, challenge, fervently appeal, and comfort. However, until we instruct as we ought, these other aspects of ministry will be largely ineffective. A solid base of Bible doctrine must be laid if we hope to lead our people out into the depths of Christian experience.

Fourth, we must give vital attention to spiritual maturation. It is fundamentally important that we understand the biblical principle expressed perhaps most clearly in Ephesians 4:11-12. There the apostle Paul speaks of the gifts which the risen Christ has given to the churches. He lists these as being apostles, prophets, evangelists, pastors, and teachers. Most Bible students hyphenate the last two, which would indicate that there is one gift involved here, that of pastor-teacher.

Now notice the reason for this as expressed in verse 12. The King James Version reads as follows, "For the perfecting of the saints, for the work of the ministry, for the edifying of the body of Christ." However, if you will compare this with a more modern translation, you will detect a very important difference. The sense of this statement is as follows, "For the *equipping* of the saints, *unto* the work of the ministry, for the edifying of the body of Christ." The purpose for which Christ gives these gifted men to the church is for the equipping or the maturation of the saints, so that the saints can perform the work of the ministry. This emphasis fits nicely with the words of Paul in 2 Timothy 2:2 when he wrote to Timothy, his son in the faith. "The things that thou hast heard of me among many witnesses, the same commit thou to faithful men, who shall be able to teach others also." The end result of this teaching-preaching ministry of the church will be that God's people are equipped or matured to the task of the ministry.

A bit later in this chapter we will talk about evangelism in the local church. But we anticipate that discussion very briefly by suggesting that the primary purpose of the meetings of the church is not to evangelize the lost. Thank God if the unsaved come to our church services and meet the Lord. We ought to be prepared to reach them wherever we find them. But the primary objective of the worship services of the church is designed, according to Scripture, to prepare the saints of God so they can effectively carry on their God-appointed witnessing ministry. This ought to be the goal toward which our entire church meeting program is aimed. And such a goal will provide the highest kind of motivation for a Christian minister. Why should we complain if our churches are not crowded with sinners? Why not accept the opportunity of using the services of the church as a dynamic avenue of ministry to our people so they will be equipped and prepared for their work?

An additional word is in order concerning services in the smaller church. They will doubtless be less formal than services in the larger city church, and this is generally desirable. The church must always seek to fit itself into the culture of the people who make up the church. However, our services must be kept free from anything that might mark them as coarse or uncouth. In our desire to be acceptable to the people there is danger that we go too far in the opposite direction and deprive the service of its proper dignity and its spirit of worship. Remember, we are redeemed sinners coming into the presence of a holy God. We should indeed respond to our Redeemer with glad and joyous hearts. But this does not allow for physical excesses or thoughtlessly arranged services.

However, our public worship could be a great deal more meaningful than is customary, and the minister should set himself to the task of making it so. To begin with let him inspire as much group participation on the part of his people as possible. In most cases the congregation comes to the house of God prepared to sing (and that half-heartedly), give some money in the offering, and listen to a sermon. This mold must somehow be broken out of if we are to recapture the spontaneity which is our birthright. It may help to have the Scripture read responsively if you are not in the habit of doing so. Or you may read "cooperatively." To read "cooperatively," the pastor announces the Scripture passage, then reads the first verse while various ones from the congregation read the remaining verses. There is no predetermined selection of participants, but the ones who have Bibles with them will each read the verse they particularly feel led to read. Sometimes there may be a momentary pause in the reading but in most cases the individuals follow each other in regular order and so complete the passage. It is an inspiring experience, permitting much more individual participation in services than otherwise. Beyond this, other original means can be used which will be effective. Special singing, testimonies, spontaneous prayers, all will help to make our worship services inspiring and helpful.

EVANGELISM

The church as a fellowship of believers shoulders a responsibility—the task of evangelism. But let us understand the relationship between the church and this responsibility. As I have previously observed, the motto, "The supreme task of the church is the evangelism of the world," is one of those slogans that has in it so very much that is true, and yet is so capable of misinterpretation. This motto, I am afraid, has given rise to the idea that the church as an entity is responsible for world evangelization. But the task of world evangelization is not so much the task of the corporate impersonal body, as it is the task of the individual Christian. The local church comes into direct confrontation with this task, in its responsibility to equip and mature the saints for the work of witnessing. In this connection, the local church is profoundly important. The universal church, the body of Christ which is a mystical spiritual entity, could never do the work of evangelism if it were not for the fact that in the local fellowship of believers this spiritual body becomes visible. Thus, the local church plays a preeminently important role in the task of world evangelism. This responsibility can be discharged in several directions.

MASS EVANGELISM

There is a place in the local church for mass evangelistic efforts. We ought not to view this method as the only way to evangelize the lost, nor even the most effective way. But we ought not to discount the fact that, particularly in rural areas, mass evangelistic efforts are still an effective means of reaching men for Jesus Christ.

VISITATION EVANGELISM

The church has another means of evangelism open to it as a church, and this is visitation evangelism. Visitation evangelism is a ministry systematically planned by the officers of the church and executed by the people in the church. It does not take the place of personal evangelism, which will be discussed a bit later, but is an additional ministry through which the church is able to reach people in their homes. To function effectively the community should be divided into areas, and teams of Christians assigned to each area. After the community is covered in this manner, specific needs will become apparent and individuals can be designated to visit those who are interested, sick, or under conviction. An aggressive pastor who is able to lead his people will be able to accomplish much through the avenue of visitation evangelism.

PERSONAL EVANGELISM

Personal evangelism is not so much a prescribed church program as it is a spontaneous, unofficial activity on the part of a truly born-again, Spirit-filled, compassionate believer. The cause of the church's tragic plight today lies in our failure at this point, and conversely the remedy lies in leading our people in this work of personal witnessing.

Somehow we have so circumscribed our evangelistic activity that we fail almost completely in breaking through the barriers that separate us from our neighbors. Just as most Christians are unfamiliar with the inner workings of the secret lodges in our towns, though we may know the members of these lodges well enough in private life, so most unevangelized people are totally ignorant of what constitutes our church life and fellowship and could not care less! They simply ignore us! For this reason it is absolutely necessary that we meet people on an individual, personal, and private level, and lead them to Christ *there*. The problem of getting them into our church fellowship will then be considerably easier.

As we exercise ourselves in this ministry, we are really obeying the heart of the great commission. "The great commission, therefore, when we sum it up, is a personal command to every Christian to go into every nook and corner of his personal world, and seek, by witnessing the power of the Holy

Spirit to the good news of God's saving grace through the shed blood of Christ, to win every lost soul in his personal world to salvation."[1]

We have not done this! W. Curry Mavis comments on our reluctance:

> Some churches, like individual persons, have agoraphobia. People with this complex have a fear of out-of-doors. They feel safer in the enclosures of their own homes. It is the same way with churches that keep their Gospel contained within four sacred walls.
>
> The matter of taking the Gospel to sinners is the great imperative of the church. Nowhere in the New Testament are sinners commanded to go to church, but Christians are commanded to take the Gospel to the unconverted. Jesus Himself went to those in the highways and byways and He gave us the pattern for all time.[2]

The failure of our churches at this point may be the single most important reason for the increasing multitudes of un-evangelized in the world today. These millions will never be reached if we expect pastors, evangelists, and missionaries to reach them. Our only hope is a mighty revival of personal witnessing. This must begin on the local level, and the pastor must take the lead in fostering it.

WORLD EVANGELISM

Finally, the church is responsible for worldwide evangelism. Up to this point we have discussed the program of evangelism for the local church as it concerns the immediate community. But the church may not stop here. The un-reached of other lands should draw out the heart and soul of the missionary church, and this church should not rest until they share in reaching those who have never heard the gospel.

Missionaries home on furlough or under appointment should be regularly featured in the church program. This

will enable people to learn of the needs of the different countries and the efforts that are being made to meet them. Sec-
ondhand information will never take the place of firsthand
accounting of those who have been in the work. Prayer letters
should be regularly received by the individual members, and
the pastor might profitably read certain selected ones at the
midweek service. In this way the church can have a vital part
in praying for those who are ministering the gospel in distant
places.

Missions should play an important role in the church's
giving. More will be said about this later, but it must be
noted here that prayers without financial support are likely
to avail very little. Our praying will be more effectual if we
have shared our material resources as well.

The church can make an additional contribution toward
world missions by producing young folks who will go as missionaries. The pastor should make this an important part of
his ministry. Parents are responsible to give their children to
the service of Christ. Young folks must be challenged with
the task and the responsibility that rests upon them as Christians. The church needs to recognize its responsibility to en-
courage those who are called of God to specific tasks, both by
prayers and financial support. Small churches can many times
make significant contributions to the cause of missions in the
number of young people sent into Christian service. They
will thus fulfill their evangelistic responsibility at home as a
church, as individuals, and in mission fields around the world.

FINANCES

The financial program of the church is likely to produce
more than its share of problems. In reopened churches the
difficulty is especially acute. In old rural churches the handling of money is a matter of custom, and is not easily
changed. Some of these churches do not receive offerings

every Sunday, satisfied to take in only enough to meet existing needs. There is no vision of what could be done with increased giving, and generally there is the danger of misunderstanding if one says too much about stewardship. Quite often the Sunday school will function with the gifts given in the Sunday school offering, while the church struggles along on the small and infrequent church offerings. If the pastor is paid at all, it will likely be through an offering taken once or twice a month for his personal support. On the other hand, a few instances are known where the church offering every Sunday is given to the pastor—which also results in a lopsided idea of church finances, usually without any concern for missions.

We cannot immediately change habits such as these. Such changes are never easy. However, if the church is to grow, the people must be made to see the importance of scriptural practices. In some way they must catch a vision of the challenge of Christian stewardship.

Church expenditures usually fall into four categories: pastoral support, missions, general fund, and building needs. Larger churches may find this division too general but for the smaller church it will be satisfactory. The minister must surely share in the offerings of the church. Missions need to be given a prominent place in the financial picture regardless of the size of the church, and provisions must be made for items of a more general nature. In addition, a building fund should be kept active for unexpected repairs or expansion.

Now then, how shall the money of the church be channeled into these recognized categories? Instead of a full-scale budget, it may be wise to begin more simply. By means of a survey of past giving, estimate the amount of income for the months ahead. Then decide what percentage of the income is needed in the various funds: pastor's support, missions, general, and building. As a result, the following picture may begin to emerge. Sixty percent might be given to the pastor, fifteen percent to missionary needs, another fifteen percent to the general fund, and ten percent to the building fund. According to this plan the pastor would receive this percentage each month regardless of the total income. In other words, the pastoral fund would always be totally expended. The missionary responsibilities would be taken care of, and if the percentage for missions gradually built up a surplus, other responsibilities could be assumed. If it became gradually depleted, some responsibilities would have to be dropped or added income would have to be provided. The general fund would operate the same way.

There are several advantages to this program. First, it is not likely to create quite as much opposition as the usual budget, since it does not demand a certain level of giving the coming year.

Another important value is evident. In some cases the rural church is rather remiss in pastoral support, and this presents a problem for the minister. He sees the need for increased giving, knows the church would prosper if it accepted its responsibilities as it ought, and yet is handicapped in effecting a solution. If he receives his pay a certain Sunday of the month or if he gets it every Sunday, he hesitates to say too much about his personal support. Yet, if he is to be true to his calling, he must challenge the people with their responsibility.

It is right here that this plan is helpful. If the pastor receives a percentage of all the offerings, while all other church needs are also taken care of, he finds it much easier to challenge the people without being put in the unenviable position of asking for his own pay. Yet each increase in church giving also increases his support. This plan has been used in several rural churches and has been found satisfactory. Of course, if the church is ready for a budget, this is the better method of the two. But where a bona fide budget may be premature, a percentage may prove to be an adequate temporary substitute.

The pastor of the small church must recognize his responsibility in leading the people to higher levels of stewardship. There are two methods the pastor may use in seeking to do this. One is that he may emphasize church expenses and repeatedly appeal to his people to meet their obligations. The other method is the use of sound, consistent Bible instruction. The pastor, by explanation of scriptural principles, builds a basis upon which to teach New Testament giving. In the first instance, the people react against the pastor because they are persuaded that he is concerned only with "money." In the second case, they are likely to give serious consideration to the message of the Word of God and so have a receptive attitude toward the counsel of their pastor.

One rural pastor, who was caught on the horns of this dilemma, gave a series of messages on stewardship. These messages dealt with the *motive* for giving, the *measure* of giving, and the *object* of giving. The first emphasized the truth that we give because of God's gift to us; the remaining messages dealt with the proportion and reasons for our stewardship. As a direct result of these messages, the giving of the church noticeably increased.

The problem is finally reduced to this issue: Our instructions in the realm of money must have as their chief concern the glory of God. Money must not be made the major object. The spiritual life of our people, their walk with God, and their understanding of Bible truth must be our first concern. When this is as it should be, the matter of money will be more easily approached and the teaching more effective.

The program of the church, as the organization of the church, is only a method of accomplishing our goal. The goal must never be lost from view. **Evangelism, spiritual** development, the glorifying of our Lord and Saviour Jesus Christ—these goals are preeminent. Whatever helps us to reach them will be a welcome part of our church program.

8

The Pattern of Church Growth

SOME OF TODAY'S IDEAS concerning church organization and growth are not scriptural. In relation to the past, the church has allowed tradition to depose the Word of God as the final authority in church practices. In relation to the present, we have allowed the spirit of the age in its various manifestations (i.e., materialism, personal ambitions, professionalism, intellectualism) to permeate our church life. There is some truth in the charges often heard from unconverted people that the church is too concerned with organization and money, and not enough with the souls of men.

The objection will likely be raised that a discussion of church growth on a broad level falls outside the scope of our theme and should, therefore, be left to others. But this objection fails to recognize that church practices on any level can affect church practices on other levels. Therefore, the problem of church growth on the small church field will be influenced by the larger problem. Deep-seated ideas leave their mark on every stratum of church life. The young men who are going into rural pastorates are trained in the same schools as those who work in larger city churches. The same advertisements which are read by the urban pastor are also read by the man in the country. Thus, the basic principles of church life must be brought into harmonious agreement with the Word of God if our churches, both rural and metropolitan, are to grow in a natural and unforced manner.

A CLOSER LOOK AT THE PROBLEM

When we speak of "church growth," certain pictures immediately etch themselves on our minds. We will imagine that in a certain town of several thousand people there is a prominent Protestant church. The church is fully organized, its origin dating back several generations. There have been a succession of pastors, some good and some indifferent, during the intervening years. Under the consecutive ministry of these men the church has undergone a gradual, if not spectacular, growth. At the present time, this imaginary church has a membership of several hundred and a Sunday morning worship service attendance of two hundred, and boasts at least an average comparative budget.

At this point a new pastor is called by the church. He is a young man, well prepared in all respects, a graduate of a respected seminary, possessing a fine personality, winning manner, and marked pulpit ability. He takes up his new charge and enters into the work with interest. He initiates a thorough visitation program, brings church records up to modern proficiency levels, streamlines the organizational structure of the church, and injects into it a new spirit of enthusiasm. As attendance increases, the community begins to take notice of the new minister and he finds himself becoming socially prominent. Invitations to speak pour in from all sides, and the new minister soon develops into a leading community figure. All of this has a correspondingly exhilarating effect on the congregation.

As time goes on, the pastor begins to assert strong leadership in all areas of church life. The offerings become more and more a dominating factor in the services. Subtle pressure is applied to any who may lag in contributing their share to the church program. Church membership takes on new and important meanings. Every possible prospect is visited and revisited, obviously with the intent of getting them to join the church. To some in the congregation it appears that money and church membership are increasingly overshadowing the more important realities of the church's ministry.

But things continue to prosper, at least outwardly. Within a five-year period, these various and seemingly disconnected efforts have been fused into one concerted force that has accomplished remarkable results. Church membership is at an all-time high. Attendance in the Sunday morning service is filling the auditorium. The budget has been enlarged each year, until the total amount given by this church draws the attention of outsiders. The pastor has been voted a sizable increase in salary, and a new educational annex has been built to the present structure, costing thousands of dollars.

But some disturbing facts are likewise evident. There is a noted absence of spiritual maturity. Those who have been members for many years seem no nearer to the Lord than before. Those who have recently been taken in as members have not left their spiritual babyhood. In many lives there is apparently little difference between what they were and what they now claim to be. Carnal characteristics continue. Conformity to the world has not decreased. The mission burden seems to have grown weaker as the heavy financial burdens of a larger local program press upon them. While the giving of the church has increased markedly, the needy areas of ministry are not getting their share. Further, while the Sunday morning attendance continues to grow, the Sunday night service and the midweek prayer meetings are struggling along with a mere handful of faithful supporters. In short, underneath the surface of this seemingly growing church, there is much to give cause for deep concern.

Now the point at issue is this—can we honestly say that this

church is an example of real scriptural church growth? Is this
imaginary illustration the ideal for which we should strive?
Something like this is being offered to aspirants to the ministry. The imaginary pastor in this situation would be held
in high esteem by many church leaders. He would doubtless
find it easy to move on to something even more promising if
he wished to do so. The news would spread that so and so
"has really done a very excellent job of 'church building'."
Other young men would imitate his example.

But I ask again, are we justified in offering this as an example of proper, spiritual, scriptural church growth? Is this
to be the balance in which pastoral work is weighed? Is a
man successful in church building because he can point to a
substantial increase in membership, a new building, and a
superior budget?

There is surely nothing wrong with these things in themselves. No man should be criticized because his church has
grown in size and financial effectiveness, or because it has
been improved organizationally. But is it right to give these
things preeminence? Is it proper to so strongly emphasize
these *evidences* of growth that we ignore, or at least under-
emphasize the factors that cause *real* church growth?

It seems clear that many of our training institutions have
put the cart before the horse. We have been teaching men to
go out with the intent to *build churches* when we should have
trained them to go out *to win men to Christ and equip them
for effective witness*. And this does not contradict our emphasis on organization in the earlier part of this book. It is
a matter of relative values. To which aspect of our task are
we addressing ourselves with utmost vigor—building a visible
organization or creating a local spiritual fellowship of believers which will normally express itself in organizational
form?

When Paul went to Iconium, Lystra, Derbe, Philippi,

Corinth, and the other cities on his missionary journeys, he was not motivated primarily with the desire to build a church. He was striving for the edification of the body of Christ! He was constrained by *love* of Christ to preach the *gospel* of Christ so that the *body* of Christ would be formed, as a result of which local bodies of believers would gather together, creating visible organizations through which the task of evangelism would be carried on.

The result of Paul's ministry was indeed the formation of local churches, and this will be the same result of such a ministry today. But we must not hold as our primary goal the mere formal organization of a group of individuals into an entity known as a church. We must understand the divine order—the preaching of the Word of God, which in turn will result in the formation of a group of individuals into that which can rightly be called a local church. Then we can give ourselves to the task of formalizing, strengthening, and directing its life and ministry. When a "church-building" job results in this way, we have great cause for rejoicing.

All this simply means that the *organism* must take precedence over the *organization; Men* must be held in higher esteem than *money.* The *Spirit's* work in conviction and regeneration must be given right of way over *our* work in building an institution. When we allow ourselves to become engrossed with the mechanics of church life to the point where we minimize the importance of the former things, we are in gross error. The result is not a spiritual church at all but the rearing of a materialistic, formal, spiritually dead organization.

Standards by Which to Judge Church Growth

There are some guides by which we can measure true spiritual church growth—guides that will indicate to us how closely we are following the divine pattern.

SPIRITUAL MATURITY

There is the standard of spiritual maturity. Real spiritual maturity in a local fellowship will manifest itself in several different ways.

1. *Ability to self-govern.* According to the Word of God, when a group of believers is truly mature in the spiritual sense of the word, they are given by the Spirit the ability to govern themselves in a scriptural fashion.
2. *Stewardship.* Spiritually mature Christians will realize the value of faithful, consistent giving.
3. *Loving cooperation.* A mature church will have learned the secret of proper human relations. The ability to discuss issues plainly, but without hurt feelings, is a mark of a mature fellowship.
4. *Separation.* The word of God teaches that Christians are to be separate from sin, ungodly associates, and false teachers. A mature church will have learned the practical truth of spiritual separation.
5. *Evangelism.* A mature church will be a witnessing church.

It should be said further that spirituality and maturity are not one and the same thing. A new convert may be walking in obedience to the Holy Spirit, living a life of separation from sin, and enjoying fellowship with Christ, yet not be mature. There is a period of time, long or short as the case may be, between conversion and maturity. But increasing maturity is a mark of church growth.

SPIRITUAL REPRODUCTION

Spiritual reproduction is a mark of church growth. Every believer is to exhibit the "fruit of the Spirit" as we learn in Galatians 5:22, but beyond this we are to *bear fruit* by "reproduction." Jesus speaks to us in these words: "Ye have not chosen me, but I have chosen you, and ordained you, that ye should go and bring forth fruit, *and that your fruit should remain*" (John 15:16, itals. added). This is a spiritual reproduction. An apple tree bears apples, a pear tree pears, and a cherry tree cherries: so a Christian is to be the means of reproducing other Christians.

This spiritual reproduction is a far cry from the church membership drives that are so prevalent. True church extension is a person-to-person, heart-to-heart proposition. It cannot be successfully diluted with salesmanship. It is a work of the Spirit through redeemed obedient hearts. Such reproduction is fruit that remains, for it is a work of God Himself.

COMMUNITY IMPACT

Another mark of spiritual church growth is community impact. Some remarkable results followed the ministry of the early church. In Acts 4, Peter and John are in the hands of the authorities as a result of their preaching and healing ministry. After the trial the writer declares that these authorities "took knowledge of them, that they had been with Jesus." There stood the man who had been healed. The miracle was evident. Peter and John had done no wrong. They were peaceful men. Yet, they were bold and forthright, showing evidence of something supernatural. The leaders were astonished. They could only observe that these men had been with Jesus. Making this kind of impact on our community may bring extraordinary results. It did for the apostles! Peter was eventually crucified! John was banished to the Isle of Patmos! James was beheaded! If we imagine that a spiritual impact on a community will always involve social acceptance, we are mistaken. But whatever the response, we must not be satisfied until the neighborhood around us becomes aware of our presence, and as a result, recognizes our relationship to the living Christ.

ENLARGEMENT

Church growth may be judged by enlargement. I have purposefully refrained from using the term "size." "Enlargement" involves size, but much more than size.

If a spiritually mature church is located in a typical community, then it will naturally become larger. This is one means of discovering whether or not we are growing. But it must not be the only criterion used. Some churches, particularly rural churches, may be in communities which, due to size, will make it impossible for the church ever to grow physically large. Other churches are in areas with a high turnover of population, with new folks constantly coming, while the ones who are reached move into other areas. The writer was a pastor of one church where this was the case. If all those who were won to Christ would have remained in the community, the size of the church would have been doubled. As it was, it increased only moderately. Because of these and similar conditions it is wrong to suggest that a pastor is not doing a good job just because the church attendance is not increasing rapidly.

Furthermore, where a church may not grow big as to its size, it can enlarge in other ways. By an increase in world mission vision the church may enlarge in a very real way in missionary extension. It can faithfully distribute funds to those who are being used of the Lord elsewhere. It can enlarge by mothering some other church in a neighboring community. Many, many churches could enlarge in this way. In fact, this type of growth probably would be far more profitable than the present trend of continually increasing local church membership rolls.

Finally, the church can enlarge by giving its youth to the cause of Christ. If mature parents and a mature pastor could form a happy partnership to help the youth of the church catch a vision of the need for spiritual service, the results would surpass comprehension. A continuous stream of dedicated young folks from our smaller churches would be a significant means of church enlargement.

These guides can help us assess in a sane, sensible way the growth of our churches. By following these standards we need not be blinded by the glitter, showmanship, and professionalism of our day. Our goals can then be kept more clearly in view and the young men who go into the ministry can do so with a clear understanding of what can properly be expected of them.

PATTERN OF CHURCH GROWTH

It remains yet to point out the pattern of activity by which such growth can be experienced. In this we simply outline some suggestions which, though not new in themselves, may induce some thought on the part of our readers and thus result in more creative activity.

Spiritual church growth is largely determined by the spirituality of its leaders. Our churches will only be what we ourselves are: what we actually are in the innermost recesses of our hearts where only God can see. It is possible to present a faultless appearance before men yet be lacking in that true inner spiritual character which is the requisite of a truly spiritual man. Without this essential the spiritual growth of the church over which we have been made overseer will be hampered. We may wonder why, may groan over the lack of progress, and may indeed be ignorant of the actual reason for the failure. But the reason is there nevertheless; and, like the underwater portion of an iceberg, it will threaten our noblest efforts with abysmal failure until it is disclosed and eliminated.

Spiritual growth in our churches is determined by the goals we set out to attain. If we desire to make a name for ourselves as the pastors of large, prosperous, influential, and socially accepted institutions, this is what we will likely succeed in accomplishing. If, on the other hand, we hold the spiritual welfare of our church to be of preeminent importance, we will find ourselves more successful in this regard. It is no secret that men usually succeed in doing what they set out to do. Therefore, let us look well to our goals. May God help us to evaluate them in the light of the Holy Scriptures and eternity, for the character and nature of our goals prophesy clearly the future course of our ministry.

Spiritual growth is experienced in exact proportion that the Word of God is the standard of our faith and practice. This statement needs little comment. Our churches must be fed on the divinely inspired Word of God.

Spiritual growth is encouraged by proper organization. This is surely not the most important factor but it is significant. There comes a time in every local church when proper, sensible organization needs to be introduced. Such organization will foster a spirit of cooperation among the members of the church, will help to eliminate the difficulties that sometimes ruffle the feelings of the believers, and will serve as an effective guide in the ministry of the church.

The danger here is failure to keep organization in its place. Organization must be seen as, in one sense, the necessary result of church growth. In another sense, it is itself a causative factor, *but only when it is first recognized as a result.* First there is the spirit, then the substance. Understood in this way, organization can indeed be one of the contributing factors to spiritual church growth.

9

The Rural Minister and His Preaching

THE RESPONSIBILITIES of a pastor are many. He must be counselor, administrator, personnel coordinator, disciplinarian, trusted friend, and instructor in the faith. Each of these responsibilities could be discussed in separate chapters, for they are all important. However, we speak here only of the pastor's pulpit responsibilities; for the task of preaching in the smaller church is so important, yet so often ignored, that we feel this aspect of his ministry deserves special attention. In fact, if the minister of the gospel will make his pulpit work what it should be, he will find it easier to exercise himself in these other ministries. If, however, he does not learn the importance of his work in the pulpit, these other aspects of his ministry will tend to be correspondingly weak. Nothing can take the place of the ministry of the Word in the local church.

THE PRIMACY OF PREACHING

This is not, broadly speaking, an age of great preachers. We have great scholars, great educators, great administrators, great diplomats, and great counselors; but we are lacking in truly great, biblical, Spirit-filled preachers. There is no lack of those who, as one country preacher once said, can "unscrew the inscrutable," but there is a dearth of those who can preach God's Word with power. In making this statement I do not speak only from my own knowledge but from that of others

87

who are wiser than I. The church is suffering because we are not "feeding the flock of God."

The greatest need in the modern pulpit is a return to Bible preaching. There has been a sad decline in the importance accorded the public exposition of the Word of God in our modern church life. Because poor preaching has almost killed the pulpit ministry, we have cast about for substitutes to fill the void and have come up with an amazing variety.

But the preaching of the Word must be given its rightful place. Paul declared that "it pleased God by the foolishness of preaching to save them that believe" (1 Co 1:21). I am aware that this should be rendered, "by the foolishness of the thing preached," but you cannot very well have something preached without the exercise of preaching. And let us not overlook Paul's counsel to Timothy to "preach the Word."

No substitute can be found for the public proclamation of the Word of God. Although other ministries can supplement the ministry of preaching, they can never replace it. Our churches will die off in direct proportion to the neglect of the exposition and application of the Word of God by our pulpits.

The Importance of Preaching in the Town and Country Churches

Somewhere the idea has been born that smaller churches do not need good preachers. Some seem to feel that people in the country are not informed on the latest thinking in theology and philosophy, therefore the rural minister can get by with a comparatively mediocre performance. It has been the practice to send young, untried men into the rural field for their "boot training," giving them something larger after they have proved themselves. Some have the idea that the rural church can subsist on the husks of our theological seminaries while the others get the kernel. Many men who were never quite able to make the grade in school, or who were just a bit eccentric or odd, are sent into the country in the hope they will be able to make the grade there. The statement, "Oh, he would be a wonderful worker in a rural church," has been made so often and with such an obvious misunderstanding of its implications that it is distressing. We need not be surprised to find our small town churches ineffective if we will not send qualified men to serve them.

The rural church needs as strong a leadership as the larger city church, for without such leadership the church is lost. To illustrate: the majority of the larger established churches have a rather long history back of them with a relatively stable membership. The members are tied to these churches by bonds of family, history, and culture. As a result, their support of the church is determined by the fact that *this is their church.* If the pastor preaches well and provides good leadership this will be an added incentive to work faithfully in it, but it is not necessarily the prime reason for doing so. The faithful member will be faithful because of the *church,* not the *minister.* If the pastor is something less than a superlative pulpiteer, these members may grumble and complain; but they usually will continue their interest.

The situation in the type of rural church we are concerned with is altogether different. There are usually very loose connections between the community resident and the church. If it is a closed church he has grown accustomed to it and so will possibly feel no compulsion to attend if it is opened. If it is a new church that is being founded the situation is even worse. This person is not constrained by habit, family ties, or custom to support this church. If he is to do so, some other motive must be found.

The fervent, sincere preaching of the gospel by the man called of God for the task is an effective means of reaching these people. Illustrations abound to prove that the man of God who preaches the Word of God with the power of God will not lack an audience to preach to. His congregation may not be large and it may not be drawn from the highest echelon of society but it will be an appreciative one. I confess to being an optimist on this point. It is my deep conviction that people will listen to the man who has a message from God.

Those preachers who are crying over the hardness of hearts and the unwillingness of people to listen to the gospel are only unveiling their own impotence. Instead of complaining, *effective preaching* let them get on their knees before God with their open Bibles before them and learn its message until it burns with white heat in their bosoms. Then let them do some practical study on the techniques of presenting a message effectively to their congregations. Finally, let them seek and find the power of the Holy Spirit for their preaching, without which no preaching will be worthwhile. Then let them enter the pulpit to declare God's eternal message and without doubt, people will come to listen.

If the rural minister will not seek to exercise an effective ministry such as this, he can expect nothing but defeat. When the most effective spokesman of the gospel can be heard on the radio or seen on TV, the rural minister need not expect to get by with careless preaching. The people will not come to listen to him. Those who have no bonds tying them to the church will simply stay at home. His audience, if he ever had any, will dwindle until it is gone. Then the poor man will wonder why he has failed, and will possibly conclude that the community is so wicked that there is no choice but to move on, and thus he probably will repeat the failure somewhere else.

ELEMENTS OF BIBLE PREACHING

What elements go together to make up effective preaching? We can do no better here than to use the definition for preaching given by the prince of Bible expositors a generation ago,

G. Campbell Morgan. In his very valuable book entitled *Preaching,* he says, "Preaching is truth through personality."[1] Further on he makes the statement that the three elements of a good sermon are truth, clarity, and passion. Let us look at them for a moment.

What shall we preach? To this there is only one answer for the man who has resolved to be a Bible preacher. He must preach the Bible. God's eternal and unchanging truth must form the basis of our message. We go even further. Not only that, but our messages must themselves be formed *from* and *by* the Bible. It is not enough to latch on to some interesting text from which to spin a web of human ideas. Our utterances must be biblical to the core. The people have one supreme need and that is to hear God's message. No one will give it to them if we do not.

Of course, one who preaches God's truth will meet many adversaries. Those who have "progressed" to the point where they can get along without God's written revelation will treat the orthodox minister as an outdated, ignorant, old-fashioned fuddy-duddy, scarcely worth the notice of this enlightened generation. Those who listen to the preaching of the Word may themselves deny it, argue against it, or declare that it does not meet the demands of this age. But in the face of these oppositions the man of God has only one recourse: Preach the Word! It is living, powerful, self-defending, and relevant. God's Book is still up-to-date and able to meet the heart need of men without Christ.

How shall we speak? Clearly, to be sure. First of all, our messages must be prepared and presented in a way most easily understood and remembered by our people. This calls for careful organization. One man may speak for thirty minutes without getting one solid, worthwhile point across. Another may speak for the same length of time, and his hearers will leave with the message clearly fixed in their minds. The reason for the difference is that the second speaker used organization. He spoke logically, outlining his points, thus impressing them upon the minds of his people. The need for clarity in preaching must not be ignored. If our people do not understand what we say, though it is said ever so eloquently, it will profit them nothing. Therefore, let the minister engage in continual study on the methods of public speaking. To learn to speak effectively is an enthralling and lifelong project.

What shall be our manner of speaking? To follow the instructions of Dr. Morgan further, let us speak passionately. Truth, though it be ever so abiding, though given ever so clearly, will still be dry as dust and utterly tasteless unless given from a passionate heart.

Some have disdained passion in preaching, suggesting that the seriousness of the message precludes an exhibition of emotion. But what is our aim in preaching? Is it not to reach man's will for the purpose of bringing him to decide for God? Why then shall we not use every means possible to accomplish the task? The defense attorney who is intent on winning the jury to his viewpoint is well aware that he must be convincing if he is to carry his point. What an impassioned appeal he makes! Why then cannot the minister of the gospel become so occupied with his message from God that his emotions and passions are affected? Why do we permit emotion in every other area of life but decry it in our Christian faith? The audience may shed alligator tears at the movies, but no one is to weep in the house of God.

Of course, it must be said and said very plainly, that mere emotion or fleshly energy is not the answer. Only that passion and inspiration which grow out of a spiritual understanding of the Word of God, a proper relationship to God through Christ by the Holy Spirit, and a sense of human need will suffice. The speaker's thoughts will thus arise from a heart that is overflowing with the divine message, his lips will speak with clarity and distinctness, and his whole being will be an instrument in the hands of the Holy Spirit, used to impress spiritual truths upon hearts. May God grant such a ministry to each of us.

CHARACTERISTICS OF BIBLE PREACHING

The biblical message *indoctrinates and teaches.* This has already been discussed in a previous chapter but it needs re-emphasis. This is one of the responsibilities of the minister of the gospel.

Bible preaching *evangelizes the lost.* A portion of the preacher's messages ought to be directed to the unsaved of his congregations, and even in those messages which are directed to the saints, sufficient gospel should be given so that any who hear can find the way. But let him not be satisfied with pulpit evangelism. He has opportunity to evangelize through personal contact as well. In fact, it may be that we are too content to execute our evangelistic responsibility solely through our pulpit ministry. This is not enough! The man in the store, the farmer in his field, the factory worker, and all others who live in the pastor's community must be reached. If they will not come to hear him he must go to visit them. This too is preaching.

Bible preaching *rebukes sin and unrighteousness.* I have never felt that a gospel minister ought to become so occupied with social wrongs that he becomes known as a reformer in the modern sense of the word, but there are times when it becomes necessary for the preacher to take a stand in public from the pulpit against sin. At such times, let him use the Word of God as a foundation from which to unmask the work of Satan.

This will be a difficult and trying task, especially for the village minister. Knowing everyone in his community, as he likely will, it may result in ruffled friendships. It is one thing to speak out against evil when its proponents are personally unknown to the minister. It is another to speak boldly and scripturally against the sins of your neighbors. Yet it must be done. It is not unscriptural to do so. It is not against the weight of historic evidence. It is not incompatible with the fundamentalist position. It must be done.

Richard Baxter, Charles Haddon Spurgeon, G. Campbell Morgan, D. L. Moody, Wilbur Chapman, and others have, along with salvation messages, exposed sin and error. God will stand with the preacher of this day who will do likewise.

Here a word of warning must be given. It is not enough to be "against" something. There is danger in imitating the preacher who preached for President Coolidge one Sunday morning. Asked by someone what the preacher preached about, "Silent Cal" replied briefly, "Sin." Asked further what the preacher said about sin, he replied, "He's against it." We must keep preeminent in our preaching the remedy to man's need, the sacrificial death, burial, resurrection, and ascension of Jesus Christ. This is the heart and core of the minister's message. "But we preach Christ." Let this be our theme, and God will anoint the message with His own power.

10

The Minister and His Community

WRITING TO THE CORINTHIAN CHURCH, Paul declares: "Now then we are ambassadors for Christ, as though God did beseech you by us: we pray you in Christ's stead, be ye reconciled to God" (2 Co 5:20). The great apostle thus recognized that the Christian, and particularly the Christian minister, fills a strategic place in God's program. In this passage we are almost stunned by the statement that the preacher of the gospel stands in the place of Christ, "in Christ's stead," pleading with men to be reconciled to God. What a position! What a responsibility!

However, while the minister holds this unique spiritual position it is also true that he is a human being, a member of a social group, and in the very process of living within this social group must deal with the same problems that beset other men. His divine appointment does not remove him from the tasks that face men who are *not* ministers of the gospel. He will be as much affected by world conditions as will his friends around him. He too will be concerned about the new school, community building, or new road that is being built in his town. The businessmen in his locality will deal with him as a businessman just as they deal with his neighbors. The preacher's family must be clothed, fed, schooled, and disciplined the same as the children of the banker, attorney, brickmason, or carpenter. All of which means that the minister, in addition to his preaching, must move among men as a man, and contact men on their level in many of their normal pursuits of life.

All of this is important to the spiritual ministry of the preacher. His community relations play a large part in determining his degree of effectiveness. He dare not ignore the value of informal contacts in the ordinary routines of daily life. In fact, he should seek in every legitimate way to assure his people that he is delighted to be a part of their community, not just an isolated voice that speaks from behind a pulpit each Lord's Day. Of all men, the rural pastor must fit into his niche as a community citizen if he hopes to reach his neighbors for Christ. As long as he holds himself aloof, looking down from his ivory tower to the people around him, he will accomplish little. While he dare not stoop to questionable practices, he must identify himself with his people.

The Minister as a Citizen

How far should a minister of the gospel go in joining his people in community activities? This has always been a nagging problem. Some ministers have negated their ministry by failing to draw a line at the proper point. Others, viewing the consequences of overinvolvement, have failed in the other direction. In either case, the preacher does not succeed in being the kind of citizen he needs to be in order to do his community the most good.

To begin this discussion, we might lay down a broad base upon which to begin. Community actions, simply because they are controlled by the community and not by the church, are not in themselves wrong. In other words, the minister of the gospel need not harbor an uneasy conscience at community exercises just because the Bible is not read and prayer is not offered.

On the other hand, it must also be said that this does not

give the minister the right to participate in *all* community activities, even though they may not be wrong in themselves. The fact that an activity is not essentially evil is insufficient reason for a Christian's involvement. Other factors must be considered besides the matter of simple right or wrong.

It appears that the minister of the gospel must be governed by several practical considerations in deciding just how deeply he will involve himself in community affairs.

First, is the thing essentially good or bad? A fireman's ball is usually no place for any Christian, let alone a minister. On the other hand, a PTA picnic on Saturday afternoon might be quite acceptable.

Second, even though the thing itself may not be evil, the question of its implications must be faced. What will be the result both to the minister and the church? How will the work of the Lord be affected? Could it be that the unchurched might get the wrong impression of the Christian life? Might people be prejudiced against the church because of the minister's choice? Perhaps it would be well for the pastor to discuss some of the concerns with the members of his congregation, especially if he is new in the community.

Third, what effect will the minister's engagement have upon his primary calling? If he is not careful, he may spend so much time on extracurricular activities that private prayer, personal devotions, Bible study, and visitations are neglected. Almost every small town has one preacher who wants to be "all things to all men," who runs to every tea party in town, umpires the ball games, meets with all the civic clubs and then wonders why he has no power in the pulpit. This danger must be shunned like the plague.

A few more things should be said on the positive side. There are effective ways by which a minister may become a vital part of his community without always doing something. It is actually as much a matter of attitude as anything else.

One need not *do* things just to prove you are a part of the community. Just resolve to *be* a part and you will discover that almost imperceptibly you are accepted as one of the people.

Exercise your right of franchise in local elections. Acquaint yourself with those who are running for local office and let it be known that you are concerned about the quality of your elected representatives. Take an active interest in PTA. The minister should be as much concerned about public school functions as others. Fit into the local community practices as much as possible. Most localities have traditional activities that are dear to the hearts of the people. For instance, in some communities it is the custom for neighbors to visit the home where a death has occurred and stay with the bereaved family through the night. This would be a good opportunity to get acquainted with the people and learn to know them in a way otherwise impossible.

As a minister of the gospel, you are dedicated to meeting the spiritual needs of the folks who live around you. Remember, therefore, that those people must first be confident that you are a friend and a trusted counselor. A convicted sinner or a troubled saint will likely avoid you until sure that you are sincerely concerned about them.

The Minister as a Businessman

The average person considers the minister a poor businessman. Whether this stems from the fact that some folks think a minister enters the ministry because he is unable to do anything else or whether it is the result of careless business practices is not clear.

And yet the minister of the gospel is forced to be a businessman. He must often act in this capacity in the interest of the church as well as handle his own personal finances, which in many cases is a **superhuman task.** Some men have had valuable business experience before entering the ministry and this has equipped them for their responsibilities. Others have not had such experience and consequently have run into difficulty. Problems therefore arise because of carelessness or incompetence. Happily, there are very few instances of clear dishonesty among preachers.

Several suggestions may be helpful. First, the importance of the minister's business relationship must be underscored. Insofar as outsiders are concerned, the minister will either be accepted, tolerated, or despised as a result of his business practices. Many shopkeepers are long-suffering with pastors, and go out of their way to help them. This makes it easy to take advantage of their good nature. But we must be careful not to abuse these privileges. Bills should be paid promptly and business affairs kept in control, that the name of the Lord not be dishonored.

Of course, it is easier to say this than to do it. Very few preachers deliberately try to evade payment of bills, but it appears that there are many who are careless in handling bills which they cannot pay. The problem is, what shall we do when we find ourselves in straitened financial circumstances, unable to pay the bill we admittedly owe? Perhaps all of us have been at this point one time or another.

Face up to the problem! If you cannot meet an obligation, do not resort to wishful thinking. Artful dreaming will not remove the difficulty. The problem exists and something must be done about it. Begin by going immediately to your creditor and explaining the situation to him. Spare no details as you tell him of your problem. Make it clear to him that you want to pay him and you will pay him just as soon as possible. Give him an approximate date upon which you hope to do so. Then if you cannot do all you hoped to do by that date, go to him again and assure him that you are doing your best and will continue to do so until the obligation is met. Businessmen will be surprisingly helpful if they are persuaded that a customer is doing his best to meet his obligations. But they can become understandably irritated otherwise.

Furthermore, learn to economize! Ministers of smaller churches often sacrifice admirably for the sake of the gospel, but further cuts in living expenses can usually be made. Money is sometimes unwisely handled, and unnecessary expenditures are made which help to bring on financial crises. Below are some questions the minister might ask himself as he considers ways of curtailing expenses:

1. Do I take a daily paper? Why? Is it essential?
2. To how many secular magazines am I subscribing?
3. Do I buy things that I do not need simply because they are "on sale?"
4. Am I careful about the use of electricity?
5. If I heat my own home, do I use fuel judiciously?
6. Do I buy unnecessary food items in addition to the essential staples, or do I purchase more expensive commodities than required?
7. Do I buy the less expensive cuts of meat or the more choice pieces? (Some of the least expensive items on the meat stand are the most valuable to proper diet balance.)
8. Have I tied myself down to burdensome monthly payments for appliances, luxuries, or a late model auto? If so, can I sell one or more of these items and so alleviate the stress?

From these questions it will be seen that economies are often possible and such economies will favorably affect your financial circumstances.

Even so, the minister may not be able to solve his problem. It may be necessary to take some secular employment for a temporary period. If the church he serves is unable to provide for him, and if insufficient help comes from outside sources, he may have to assume a secular job to make financial ends meet. This does not imply that the preacher must stop preaching and leave the ministry. It will be possible in the majority of cases to continue his ministry while working for a time. There is no harm in a preacher working to support his family in addition to his preaching. It will not lower him or his position in the eyes of the community. In fact, he may find himself commended for it.

One rural pastor had to take temporary employment with a local businessman because of insufficient income. An attorney in the local town was rather well acquainted with this pastor and held him in high esteem. On one occasion the minister was at the top of a long extension ladder when the attorney passed by on the street below. He recognized the preacher and with a friendly wave of the hand passed on. Some days later the lawyer met the preacher in a local store and commended the minister for his willingness to work. His statement went something like this: "I was delighted to see a minister of the gospel mingle with the common man for a change, as you did the other day. I commend you for it. More people would take an interest in Christianity if they would see more evidence of a real concern on the part of the ministers. I know a minister is a busy man but when he refuses to interact with people around him, he loses the touch that will make him effective." These words, by the way, were spoken by a man who was a respected member of a very large church.

There is a possibility, of course, that the minister will find it impossible to work and continue his ministry at the same time. If so, then he has no choice but to leave the pulpit, at least temporarily, and maintain his financial solvency. If he does this, he likely will have occasion to take up his ministry at some other time and place. On the other hand, if he makes shipwreck of his finances, he may never again be given the opportunity of service.

Both the minister and church are blemished when the pastor leaves town with unpaid bills. The situation need not go this far to become disgraceful. Indebtedness cannot always be avoided but when the obligations begin to rule the man instead of the man ruling the obligations, the danger point has been reached.

The Minister as Husband and Father

The home life of the minister is his most potent instrument for good in the community, yet the one aspect of his life that is too often ignored. A godly home life will speak volumes to a spiritually needy community. Yet this is frequently the point at which the minister's testimony is weak. It is a sensitive problem to handle! After all, a man's home is his castle, and people in any home dislike having their most intimate affairs discussed by someone else. Many a traveling minister has found himself in a preacher's home that was a good deal less than ideal, yet his mouth was sealed and rebuke seemed impossible. For this reason it appears proper to take this opportunity to say a few things that desperately need saying.

Consider the importance of the home. I refer here not to its importance within the context of a minister's life and testimony but to its importance as an institution. As such it antedates all others—nations, schools, and churches. The home was born when man was created and grew along with the human family.

The importance of the home as an institution cannot be overemphasized. It has well been said that "the hand that rocks the cradle is the hand that rules the world." Homes are the strength of any nation. Homes are the basic unity of society. The strength of our society must be the strength of our homes or we have no strength. If our homes are founded and developed according to the teaching of the Word of God, then our schools, churches, and nations will likewise take on a proper character.

It is clear then that the minister of the gospel ought to accept as one of his chief responsibilities the fostering of Christian homes. His ministry should be aimed at instructing the young, counselling the betrothed, and aiding those involved in marital difficulties. The best possible way to make the *people* in his church or community what they ought to be is to make their *homes* what they ought to be. If he can succeed in establishing his people in their home life they will more likely grow into mature, fruitful, and godly Christians.

But many otherwise sincere ministers are unable to do this. Though sound in the faith, these preachers exhibit serious deficiencies in their own homes and this handicaps their ministry. If the pastor himself has not experienced the reality of a scriptural home life, he will be unable to lead his people into it. We are unable to lead our people higher than we ourselves have gone.

There is an additional facet to the matter. He will not only be impotent in leading his people in this one sphere, but his failure in his own home will in some degree or other curtail the effectiveness of his entire ministry. If he does not love his wife "as Christ also loved the church, and gave himself for it" (Eph 5:25), he need not be surprised if his people grow cold in their love for God. If his wife does not subject herself to her husband "as unto the Lord," he must not be irked if the church is unsubmissive to Christ. If he does not establish a proper home atmosphere, his flock cannot be expected to do so. If the pastor allows objectionable reading matter in his home, he cannot crusade from the pulpit against the smut on the news stand, nor can he rebuke his people simply because they go a bit further in their reading material than he. If his children are disobedient to their parents and rebellious against God, he cannot preach with conviction against the sin of his congregation or his community. If his own offspring is unsaved, he will be handicapped in seeking the salvation of the children of others.

The home of the minister of the gospel must, by the grace of God, be a model after which the folks in his community can pattern their homes. To this the Word of God gives clear testimony. Paul says that a minister of the gospel must be one who "ruleth well his own house, having his children in subjection with all gravity; (For if a man know not how to rule his own house, how shall he take care of the church of God?) " (1 Ti 3:4). The household of the man of God must give evidence of being molded by a scriptural pattern, otherwise he has no right to instruct the people of God.

The minister's home should evidence the following characteristics if it is to represent a truly biblical home:

1. The relationship between husband and wife should be marked by understanding and love. The husband is the head of the home and should exercise this responsibility. The wife is subject to her husband and should lovingly take this place of subjection. For more enlightenment, read the instructions in Ephesians 5, Colossians 3, and 1 Peter 3.

2. The Bible should be the standard for the home. Individual devotions should be the practice of all adults and older children, and family prayers ought to be a habitual practice.

3. Children must be taught obedience. Somewhere in life an individual must face the matter of authority. It is futile to imagine that we can do away with authority by rejecting "authoritarianism." A man will meet and grapple with the problem of authority either in the home,

the school, society, or in the hard, ruthless, and unbending circumstances of life. At one point or another a person will learn that things cannot always go his own way. What better place to instill this truth than in the home. Here the minds of the children are in a formative stage, the wills are not so decisively set and training is possible. "Fathers, provoke not your children to wrath: but bring them up in the nurture (training) and admonition (teaching) of the Lord" (Eph 6:4).

4. The house itself should be physically clean. Some wives are, of course, more proficient in housekeeping than others but the art can be acquired by all. Some may argue that this is solely within the province of the woman. We reply in turn that if the husband will take the place in the home that is his by divine decree and exercise his responsibility, the situation is rare when the wife should not respond in a desirable manner. At least until the husband has done his part, he has no right to lay the blame on his wife.

The home of the minister of the gospel, if these characteristics are in evidence, can be a powerful means of evangelism. Young folks who do not know the meaning of a good home life will find their way into his home and resolve that their own home shall be patterned after it. Those contemplating marriage will have held before them a living picture of God's ideal. Parents who have not been taught the Word of God concerning the home will mingle with this godly family and perhaps through this fellowship come to know the Lord for themselves. Such a home may well reach far out beyond the confines of its immediate locality, to the blessing of thousands of lives.

But what if the home is lacking? What if the minister, while preaching a gospel message and sincerely seeking to win souls to Christ, neglects his own home life? What if his children, instead of developing into useful adults, go through their teens without becoming Christians and end up spiritual renegades? What if, instead of being a blessing, the home of the minister becomes a curse? What can *such* a home do for God? May the Lord help us as ministers and missionaries to make our homes what God would have them!

Yes, the minister of the gospel has a community responsibility. The town and country minister especially so! He must learn the importance of these relationships, and then discharge these responsibilities in such a manner that his service will be ennobled and strengthened rather than shriveled and weakened.

11

The Priority of Love

THE STORY IS TOLD of a young minister who asked an older pastor friend to name the one most important requirement for a successful pastoral ministry. The wiser and more experienced gentleman replied, "Love your people." This is our theme for the final chapter of this book. If a minister of the gospel expects to be effective, he must indeed *love his people*.

LOVE IS ESSENTIAL

It is important in any type of work. The professor in the classroom, the evangelist, the youth worker, the urban pastor —all must possess this quality. However, for the small town pastor it is an absolute "must." If this is lacking, the ministry will fail.

Its importance cannot be overstated. Throughout this discussion we have insisted on various techniques that will help the pastor to be more effective. These techniques are important. What is said in this closing chapter must not be taken as a neat attempt at backtracking. Organization, programming, preaching, visitation, and other activities are all parts of the total ministry. But when we have said all this, we are forced to the conclusion that a deep, personal love for the people whom we serve is the one inescapable essential. I have known Christian workers, lacking in some apparently im-

portant abilities, who nevertheless were greatly used of God
because they served in a spirit of love. But I have never observed anyone, regardless how talented or able, who was successful without love.

We must at this point define our terms. Sometimes we
profess to love the *souls* of people but not necessarily the *individuals themselves.* This is not love! It is not sufficient to
love our people for what God is able to make of them. We
must love them for what they are NOW. Our people will
know the difference!

There is always the tendency to react to a spiritually needy
group of people something like this: "How far from God these
people are! How desperately they need the gospel! How
great is their sin! We must give them the gospel." And so we
proceed to preach the gospel. We warn them of their sin. We
detail to them the judgments of God. We denounce them in
fiery language. We boldly preach the only way of salvation.
We tell them that they will be lost unless they accept the
message of salvation.

And then what? Then we declare, "Now I've told them.
They have the gospel. They have heard. If they are not
saved, it is not my fault."

But are we certain it is not our fault? With such an approach, we leave the distinct impression that we are concerned
enough to throw a rope in their direction but not concerned
enough to get ourselves wet. In short, we don't really love!

If this one essential could become vital to us, what changes
would occur! How much more earnestly would we labor!
And who can doubt that the response would be accordingly
greater?

This may perhaps explain some tragic failures in Christian
work. It is my conviction that some of those who fail in their
task, while apparently possessing all necessary equipment, may
be wanting at this point. They love their work but not their

people. They are sound in the faith but lacking in love. They are substandard in that one ingredient which touches the hearts of their hearers.

The tragedy is that this lack is almost imperceptible until the minister actually gets into the work. Mission boards, denominational leaders, and pulpit committees may resort to every conceivable method of weeding out undesirables, but this is one problem which is usually beyond discernment until it is too late. The only alternative is to challenge prospective ministers with its importance, relying upon the Spirit of God to create within them the necessary concern for those to whom they are called to minister.

LOVE IS SCRIPTURAL

What I propose here is not simply good psychology. I do not advocate this Spirit-born love for souls simply because it brings success. There is a deeper reason. The Word of God itself recognizes its importance. Among the many passages to which we could turn, we refer to Philippians 2:20, where Paul says concerning Timothy, "For I have no man likeminded, who will naturally care for your state." Paul is sending Timothy to the Philippians because he is the only one who *cares*. That word is interesting. Vine's *Expository Dictionary of New Testament Words* says that it "signifies to be anxious about, to have a distracting care." Further study reveals that this word is the very same one used by Christ in Matthew 6:25, 28; 10:19; and Luke 10:41; and by Paul in Philippians 4:6. In each of these cases, warning is given against being "anxious." Believers are not to "take thought" for their food and raiment. They are not to "take thought" concerning their defense when brought before the authorities. Martha was chided by the Lord for being "careful and troubled," and Paul bluntly declares, "Be careful for nothing." The exhortations are not urging the believers not to have normal care and concern in the affairs of life. They speak rather of that distracting care that belies faith in a loving heavenly Father.

But what a seeming contradiction! Paul turns directly around and observes that Timothy is the only one he can send to the Ephesians, since he naturally *cares* for their state. In other words, he is troubled and distracted for their spiritual welfare. He is anxious concerning their state in Christ. So Paul sends him to Ephesus.

How are we to harmonize these two emphases? There is a very simple answer. Some time ago a preacher properly observed that, "We are everywhere instructed not to be anxious about *things*, but we are plainly exhorted to be anxious about *people!*" And since Timothy possessed this consuming, distracting love for people, Paul considered him the best possible choice to send to Ephesus.

This throws light on another problem. Many Bible expositors agree, on the basis of internal evidence, that Timothy was by nature seemingly unfitted to serve as successor to the great apostle Paul. His physical constitution was apparently not robust, nor was he bold and aggressive in dealing with the problems of administration in the church. Bishop Moule suggests that Timothy was "shy and sensitive even to timidity, anxious in the face of difficult duty, clinging to a stronger personality than his own, born rather to second . . . than to lead."[1]

Knowing all this, the question has arisen as to why Paul chose Timothy for an obviously important position. Was Paul no better judge of character than that? Did he have no stronger leader than Timothy to assign to the church at Ephesus? But right here Philippians 2:20 comes into focus again: "For I have no man likeminded, who will naturally care [be anxious about] for your state." Paul was saying, "I am sending you the very best I have. I am sending you the person who possesses the one requirement for the gospel ministry. I am sending you a man who loves you. Here is a man who will allow himself to be used as God wills for your spiritual benefit."

Paul knew Timothy from the time of his childhood. He was acquainted with each quirk of his personality, each weakness of his nature, every inadequacy of his temperament. If the apostle was willing to sacrifice other and generally necessary virtues for the sake of this one prerequisite, ought not we to take special note and seek it in our own ministries?

Love Is Practical

This love we speak of is not theoretical. Love can never exist without expression. True love between husband and wife, between parents and children, between brothers and sisters, will always act for the good of the person loved. Love must always manifest itself in tangible acts of kindness. It is not less true of the love of God's servants for others. The love which Timothy expressed for the Ephesians and the love which we profess to have for our fellowmen must translate itself into practice or it indicts itself as spurious.

While this practical outworking of love must be a spontaneous thing, it will not be out of order to suggest some ways by which the pastor or Christian worker can make this love practical. One of the most effective methods of reaching friends for Christ is through our own homes. Assuming that the Christian worker has a home that is fitted for the task, the opportunity exists for a most effective witnessing effort. The approach must be informal. There is no preaching. There is no "church service." The home is simply used as a medium through which you and your unreached friends can meet on common ground.

A good way to begin is to invite a neighboring family to your house for a meal. For this purpose, do not invite someone who is already a member of your church or who is already on intimate terms with you. Choose someone who has never shown any particular interest in you or your church and in whose home you never have been invited as a guest. Set the date long enough in the future so your friends are confident of the sincerity of your invitation. When the time of the appointment arrives, make the home as cheery and relaxed as possible. Help your guests to feel as much at ease as possible.

Spend the evening in constructive but general conversation. Endeavor to establish a compatible relationship between you and your guests. Do not press your Christian convictions upon them immediately. It is doubtful if any direct effort at evangelism should be made at all in the beginning, though there may be cases where effective work can be done at the start. This is not likely, however. It is better to close the evening with a warm period of devotions, then permit your friends to depart. Such a contact will open the door for further visits, and this in turn shortly will make it possible for you to leave a positive testimony for Jesus Christ.

This type of Christian service never has been properly explored. It is inconceivable that neighbors would remain aloof if Christians would seek in this way to break down the barriers that divide. If the servants of Christ would engage regularly in this practice, they would see victories that are almost beyond belief. How easy it would be to witness to folks about Christ if we would bring ourselves together on one level!

One Christian couple moved into a needy community and began work in just this way. For the first six months, no effort was made to conduct church services. When the first services were held (in the couple's living room) the attendance jumped almost immediately in the 60s and 70s. A healthy work is well on its way because someone used his home to win souls.

How does this fit into our theme? Because a spiritual love

of souls is necessary if we would serve others in this way. Let us honestly face facts! Many Christians, even many Christian pastors, would not engage in this type of witnessing for the simple fact that it is too much trouble. Furthermore, we might end up with a socially objectionable character in our home and this we will not have. We lack the essential ingredient of love.

Or take the idea of helpfulness in times of need. The small town pastor will have many opportunities to meet everyday needs in the lives of his people. Someone will become ill and have to be taken to the hospital or doctor. Another becomes ill at home and needs assistance with the housework. A farmer suffers an accident with the result that he can no longer do his chores. A community resident must transact some necessary business in town but needs a car in order to go. It is the privilege of the minister to help these people and so manifest the spirit of God.

Someone may object that people will take advantage of our good nature and thus become social parasites. Sadly enough, this is true. And we must recognize that there are limits beyond which one ought not go, since there is the danger of undermining the self-reliance of the people themselves. But the minister who is moving among his flock with a heart like that of Jesus Christ will rather go too far than not far enough. He will prefer to do too much for fear of doing too little. This characteristic of love has been described in many ways. Hannah Moore wrote: "Love never reasons, but profusely gives; gives like a thoughtless prodigal its all, then trembles lest it has done too little." As Henry Ward Beecher expressed it, "We never know how much one loves, until we know how much he is willing to suffer and endure for us: it is the suffering element that measures love."

The apostle Paul exhorts: "Let this mind be in you, which was also in Christ Jesus." Upon this there follows the re-

counting of the greatest experience of suffering for the sake
of love in all recorded history. Surely if this mind of Christ
is indeed our mind we will be moved with the same com-
passion.

This in turn will enable us to meet every spiritual need of
our people. The pastor who loves his flock with a love like
that of Christ will be able to "reprove, rebuke, exhort" without projecting animosity and ill will. He will speak, "the
truth in love" and his message will be honored. It has been
said by many pastors that they do not feel free to speak about
certain subjects because of the reaction it would produce
among the people. Therefore, evangelists and visiting speakers
are brought into the church to speak to the people about
matters that the pastor himself feels unable to cope with.

Certainly there should be visiting speakers in our churches.
But the pastor who really loves his people will not need to
hire someone to preach to the specific needs of his congregation. He can speak the message God gives him with love and
concern and leave results with God. If they refuse to heed
him, they will not listen to any other, for the one who loves
you and knows you can speak to you more frankly than the
one whom you scarcely know. Therefore, I echo the words of
the old pastor quoted in the beginning of the chapter, "Love
your people!" And loving them, serve them!

Appendix A

Guide for Adopting a Church Constitution

THIS SPECIAL SECTION is added for the purpose of providing assistance to the uninitiated in forming a church constitution. The method is as simple and uncomplicated as it can be made. The reader will note that we do not actually offer a sample constitution. For this there is good reason. First, to draw up a constitution without using an actual church as a model makes it more or less theoretical and of little use. But to draw up a constitution using an actual church as an example will make the sample constitution so exclusive that other churches will find it difficult to adapt it to their own situations. Therefore, here are listed only the main articles of a normal constitution, and under the articles the matters that should be clarified are indicated. With this help, the rural minister can proceed to form a constitution which will be organizationally proper yet tailored to the needs of the specific group.

First, there is the preamble, which generally sets forth the reasons for organizing the group and may give a brief historical sketch of incidents which led to the origin of the church. Following the preamble, the articles will be listed, designated by roman numerals and located in the middle of the page as will be seen later. Under each article are the paragraphs which deal with separate phases of the article, each of these to be called sections. The sections under the articles will be enumerated.

ARTICLE I—NAME

The name of this church shall be _____

ARTICLE II—AFFILIATION

(The status of this church in relation to other churches or groups of churches must be clarified under this article. Will the church be a member of a denomination, in fellowship with an association of independent churches, or totally independent of all organizations? This article must state which.)

ARTICLE III—PURPOSE

(Here the purpose of the group must be declared. What is the church seeking to do? What are its goals? Since most fundamental churches exist for the same purpose, this article may be similar in most constitutions.)

ARTICLE IV—FINANCES

(How will the church raise money? Will church suppers, bazaars, rummage sales, professional fund drives, or free-will tithes and offerings be utilized? It is essential that this be clearly defined.)

ARTICLE V—DOCTRINAL STATEMENT

(The church may choose to adopt a doctrinal statement from some other group, or may prepare one of its own.)

ARTICLE VI—GOVERNMENT

(Under this Article are the following specifications for the organizations within the church:

A. Distinguish between the various organizations, such as Sunday school, youth group, and so on. In larger churches these groups all have their own constitutions, but in smaller ones it is admissible to designate each one in the church constitution and clarify its purpose and activity.

B. Explain the different offices in these organizations: who shall govern them, and what titles shall be used for the leaders.

C. State the qualifications of those who shall be candidates for these offices. These qualifications should be set forth in detail.

D. State whether these officers are elected or appointed, and who is to do the electing or appointing.

E. Designate the length of service of these officers, and whether or not they can succeed themselves in office.

F. Give directions for removal of unqualified persons from office.

The outline under this article should be in three sections, dealing with (1) *the ministry,* (2) *official boards,* and (3) *subsidiary organizations.* If there is a *trustee board,* as well as an official church board, then there would be four sections under Article VI.)

ARTICLE VII—MEMBERSHIP

(Here the questions of who shall be members, qualifications for membership, the process by which one becomes a member, how to remove one from membership, and voting age must all be answered.)

ARTICLE VIII—MEETINGS

(This article usually deals with the business meetings of the church—primarily their frequency, who is to chair them, how they are to be called, and how the business is to be presented and transacted. It must also be stated what voting majorities are necessary for adoption of a measure.)

Article IX—Fiscal Year

(Will the fiscal year conform to the calendar year? If not, specify the termination point.)

Article X—Amendments

Article XI—Dissolution Clause

(Standard copies of this clause can be secured from most church and mission board offices.)

Appendix B

The 1970 Census and Rural America

THE QUESTION of the relative significance of rural America in contrast to urban America may legitimately be raised, in light of the present sociological and political climate. For this reason, it seems wise to offer a few comments concerning the size and importance of the evangelistic task facing the church in rural America.

Our disenchantment with the needs of rural America can be traced largely to our current habit of thinking in terms of percentages. In 1960, for example, the percentage of people living in rural America was around 35 percent of the population. This was significantly lower than in 1950, when approximately 40 percent were living in rural America. Now we view the statistics of the 1970 census[1] and discover that a little less than 30 percent of our people are rural residents. The resulting impression is one of rural disintegration and decay.

However, when you look at this from the standpoint of numbers rather than percentages, the picture is not quite the same. The thirty-five percent rural population in 1960 resulted in a numerical figure of about 60 million. In 1970, the percent of rural population of our 200 million-plus remains at about 60 million. The *number* of people in rural America over the past several years has thus remained quite constant, though the *percentage* of people in rural America as related to urban America has been steadily decreasing due to the rapid rise of population in urban USA. To put it another way, we had 60 million people in rural America and about the same number of people in rural America in 1970.

Occasionally, the TV news media will portray the desolate, despairing story of a rancher in some remote part of our country who is finally selling out, after a long life of rural residence. The creaking gate, the sagging porches, the decrepit surroundings, all tell the story of decay and death. There are some isolated cases just like this. However, if anyone questions the continuing vigor of rural USA, he need only travel throughout the length and breadth of the country and view for himself the many rural communities that are not even close to depopulation. Many are in desperate need of an aggressive evangelistic ministry. The evangelization and church-building challenge of rural America continues even in the complex society of today.

Notes

PREFACE

1. Mark A. Dawber, *Rebuilding Rural America* (New York: Friendship, 1937).

CHAPTER 1

1. C. I. Scofield, ed., *The Scofield Reference Bible* (New York: Oxford U., 1945), p. 1021.
2. Lester Pipkin, unpublished material.
3. E. B. Andrews, quoted by Augustus H. Strong, *Systematic Theology* (Philadelphia: Judson, 1907), p. 892.
4. Lyman Abbott, quoted by ibid., p. 896.
5. Francis A. Schaeffer, *The Church at the End of the Twentieth Century* (Downers Grove, Ill.: Inter-Varsity, 1970).

CHAPTER 2

1. Mark A. Dawber, *Rebuilding Rural America*.
2. Henry K. Rowe, *The History of Religion in the United States* (New York: Macmillan, 1924), p. 61.
3. Dawber.
4. Carl A. Clark, *Rural Churches in Transition* (Nashville, Tenn.: Broadman, 1959), pp. 10-11, 12.
5. Bureau of the Census, *1970 Census* (Washington, D.C.: U.S. Government Printing Office).
6. Quoted by W. Curry Mavis, *Advancing the Smaller Local Church* (Winona Lake, Ind.: Light & Life, 1957).
7. National Association of Evangelicals, *New Churches for a New America* (Chicago: NAE).
8. William W. Sweet, *Religion in the Development of American Culture, 1765-1840* (New York: Scribner, 1952), p. 116.
9. Ibid., pp. 110-12.

CHAPTER 3

1. Carl A. Clark, *Rural Churches in Transition*, p. 107.
2. Ibid., p. 95.
3. Ibid., p. 85.
4. Ibid., pp. 108-15.
5. Ibid., pp. 111-12.
6. Ibid., p. 112.

CHAPTER 6

1. Harold F. Linamen, *Business Handbook for Churches* (Anderson, Ind.: Warner, 1957).
2. Ibid.

CHAPTER 7

1. J. E. Conant, *Every-Member Evangelism* (New York: Harper, 1922).
2. W. Curry Mavis, *Advancing the Smaller Local Church.*

CHAPTER 9

1. G. Campbell Morgan, *Preaching* (Westwood, N.J.: Revell, n.d.).

CHAPTER 11

1. H. C. G. Moule, *The Second Epistle to Timothy* (1905; reprint ed., Grand Rapids, Mich.: Baker, 1952).

APPENDIX B

1. Bureau of the Census, *1970 Census.*